www.awgp.us
All World Gaytri Pariwar
Bay Area, California USA

What is Spirituality ?

(Translation of Hindi Book: "Ādhyātma Kyā Thā? Kyā Ho Gayā? Kyā Honā Chāhiye?"by Brahmavarchas)

◈

Publishers:

Shri Vedmata Gayatri Trust (TMD)
Shantikunj, Haridwar

Third Print: 2010   **Price: Rs.** 35.00

First Edition: 2007
Third Print: 2010

ISBN: 81-8255-025-4

Price: Rs. 35.00

English Translation and compilation by
Dr. Amitabh Saraf &Dr. Rajani Joshi

Publishers:
Shri Vedmata Gayatri Trust (TMD)
Shantikunj, Haridwar,
Uttarakhand 249 411, India.

Website: www.awgp.org

Ph. 91-(0)1334-260602/261955

Abstract

Spirituality deals with enlightening one's thoughts, emotions and intrinsic tendencies. In simple terms it is the most evolved and comprehensive science of psychological, sociological and moral development, and ultimate progress. It brightens the intellect together with inculcation of sensitivity towards fellow beings and towards the grace of Nature. There is no place for superstitions, fantasy or escapism in a truly spiritual life. Spiritual progress in no way blocks scientific and materialistic progress. In fact, it gives altruistic touch and prudent directions to both so that progress will not be focused only towards increase in luxurious comforts and worldly profits; it will not enrich and empower only some privileged ones. Scientific and materialistic progress guided by spirituality would lead to a holistic growth whose benefits would reach out to the whole of humanity and which will not result in any counter-effects in future. Spirituality can and should be adopted on every front of life for elevating happiness and illuminating the future.

Preface

The domains of spiritual knowledge and practices are neither confined to abstract philosophical deliberations of some scholars, nor to some mythological narrations or rhetoric anecdotes of the lives of divine incarnations that might attract or engross the minds of devotees. Intellectually inspiring discourses and discussions, or devotional songs and stories may serve the purpose of introducing or attracting the minds of the listeners towards some spiritual teachings. But this alone is not sufficient for spiritual progress. Same is true of the religious rituals like worship. These practices would be nothing more than some different kinds (may be 'holy kinds', though) of entertainment unless one attempts to adopt the underlying teachings in one's conduct. Devotion is not some kind of hallucination or sentimental excitement. It is a process of inner linkage and eventual unification with the object of devotion. It demands surrender of ego, change of attitude, and control with positive orientation of ambitions of the devotee to match with the noble qualities of the deity.

The rituals of worship use a visible symbol of greatness, of elevated virtues – e.g. a holy picture or idol of a manifestation of God. Looking at this symbol helps in easy attention of mind. Lighting lamps and fragrant sticks in front of the deity, offering sacred water (oblation), flowers, clothes, sweets, etc, singing devotional songs, praying before it, further help positive conditioning of the mind. But this alone is not sufficient. Often it is found that 'religious minded' people regard completing of some rituals (*pūjā-pāṭha*), visiting a shrine and chanting prayers and doing some worship there on some auspicious day, taking a dip into the holy rivers and ponds, etc, as the end of fulfilling their religious duties or spiritual efforts.

Not only that, people often put a list of their demands before the deity and 'promise' doing some special kind of worship, distributing sweets of some special kind in large quantity, donating gold or money in the shrine in return. It is like a cheap trading. Is God some greedy fellow who would be bribed by someone's offerings? Is His moral system so shaky that all sins would be wiped out by simply chanting His name several hundred or thousand times, by going to pilgrimage, or offering alms etc? Certainly not! If it were so, every priest of every shrine would have become Almighty by now; there would have been no need of any ethics. No efforts, no qualities or talents would have been required to achieve great successes!

Those who think that devotion of divinity or spiritual experiments pertain only to fulfillment of some rituals and mere recitation of some sacred hymns and prayers are under false impressions. The earlier they wake up the better for them and the society.

We must remember that spiritual progress cannot commence without *tapa* and *sādhanā*. These are the most essential and adept supports for spiritual enlightenment and evolution of self-consciousness up to high realms of divinity. *Tapa* means self-restrain, penance and voluntary observance of ascetic disciplines for chiseled self-refinement. *Prāyaśchita* (atonement, expiation) is also a part of this purifying process.

It requires wholehearted altruistic service as well because one needs to do much more for the welfare of the society than the harm he has caused because of his mistakes or misdeeds. Without this he cannot get rid of the burden of his blemishes. If one digs a big hole, he would need larger amounts of soil and harder labor to fill it back. Sinful or wrong actions cannot be rectified or compensated without thorough attempts at performing compensating, benevolent deeds.

Sādhanā is a process of self-discipline, self-improvement, self-transformation and inner-ascent by individual efforts. Positive orientation of thoughts, broadening of attitude, cultivation of virtuous qualities and sincere practice for their adoption in conduct are integral parts of *sādhanā*. Yoga exercises, fasting, going for pilgrimage without comforts, etc are useful for *tapa*, which is a prerequisite for *sādhanā*. Breathing exercises of *prāṇāyāma*, practices of meditation (*dhyāna*), adoption of s*wādhyāya* (study and contemplation over the sagacious thoughts, lives and works of elevated souls), and s*atsang* (inspiring company of enlightened personalities, attending discourses of saints and spiritual gurus) lend excellent support in *sādhanā*.

In short, devout endeavors for outer and inner purity of personality, integrity of character, enlightenment of thoughts and emotions, and adoption of moral conduct and righteous deeds, are the foundations of spiritual development. Spirituality incorporates virtuous evolution and unbounded expansion of the "self". The science of spirituality is therefore no less important than any branch of science. The superiority of *chetanā* (consciousness force, life-energy and conscience) over *jaḍa* (inanimate matter) is well known. It is a conscious being that makes use of matter and not the other way round. The material based modern science deals with understanding, refining and making better use of the *jaḍa* component of Nature. But the science of spirituality edifies the consciousness, brightens the intellect to accrue the acumen to utilize the potentials of material based science adeptly for the benefit and welfare of the world. Therefore the science of spirituality assumes more important place in life than any other science.

It is well known that a perverted, deluded or devilish mind can misuse the acquired powers to ruin the world. The gamut of wonderful achievements of modern science and its enormous gifts to the modern civilization would be of no use or would be destroyed in no time if the power of science were misused. We all know the dreaded risks of environmental pollution and nuclear and biological warfare produced by the very science that has made our lives amazingly comfortable, taken us to the stars, equipped us with satellite communication and what not! The role of the 'other' science that enlightens the mind and enables its genuine control by ethical values and sagacity is therefore more vital and cannot be neglected any more.

Dormancy or devolution of the *chetan* (pertaining to consciousness) component of Nature and consequent complexities, for example, corruption and decline of peoples' thoughts, sentiments and value system lead to irreversible deterioration and degeneration of the foundation of the society. It simultaneously gives rise to varieties of problems on the health and security fronts as well. It steals away viable peace and happiness from people's life. Unfortunately, this is what seems to have been chosen as the 'folly of the wise' in our times. Negation, negligence, misconception and distortion of the science of spirituality is the severest of the flaws of our times, which needs be rectified now without any delay.

Realizing this need of the present times, seer-sage and spiritual saint Pandit Shriram Sharma Acharya pioneered renaissance of scientific spirituality in the new light. His mission of refinement of people's line of thinking via the reformative and constructive programmes of the Gayatri Pariwar has initiated an irreversible movement of eradication of blind faith, superstitions and insane customs spread since the medieval times in the fields of spirituality and religion. His mission has showed what the *rishi* culture – the divine culture of Vedic Age – was in reality and how it could be resurrected in the modern times. His exceptional brilliance, preeminent writings, eloquent orations, discourses, scientific acumen, and depth of knowledge, his saintly life, devotion to altruistic service of all beings, etc are remarkably reflected in his monumental works and stand as authentic proofs of the principal of *sādhanā se siddhi* (attainment of supramental talents by devout spiritual endeavors).

The book unfolds the true meaning, relevance and importance of spirituality and shows practical ways to adopt it in today's life.

— *Dr. Pranav Pandya, MD*

Contents

The Realms of Science & Spirituality   1

This universe is formed out of both consciousness-force and matter. The domain of learning and experimenting with matter constitutes material-based science or what we simply refer to as science in the modern times. The domain of realizing and understanding consciousness and the theory and process of its enlightened evolution pertains to (the deeper science of) spirituality. The totality, purpose, and fruitfulness of the word "science" is accomplished only in adept amalgamation of material-based science and spirituality.

Though dealings in natural sciences began way back when man discovered fire, began to rear animals, started agriculture, began to weave clothes, build homes, pots and tools etc., its visibly significant advancement took place in the twentieth century only. Machines, equipments, weapons, drugs, means of conveniences etc have been created in the twentieth century at a rate that has fast surpassed the same in any previous times.

In the twentieth century, there has been a significant increase in the interest of the common man towards material-based science. It has become an important subject in the curriculum of all higher and elementary schools as well. If modern science proceeds on ill-directed paths then there can be as much destruction as the development that has taken place over the past millennium. Though this issue is slightly out of context for the present discussion, what can be stressed is that spirituality has got left behind and ignored in the sequence of progress. It has failed to rise to an extent that could create a balance (with material-based science) like two wheels of a cart or two wings of a flying bird. Because of this imbalance alone, modern science and technology has got an opportunity to wildly encroach every walk of life and even cause widespread destruction and hazards in several ways. If both the disciplines had cooperated with each other, development would have been total and the descent of heaven upon the earth would have been possible.

Modern Science vis-à-vis Spirituality:

The basic principal of science, as we know today, is that it verifies all the hypotheses in terms of perceivable facts and evidential reasoning. Till it establishes truth by experiments and hard evidence, it neither gets satisfied, nor does it rest. All hypotheses of natural sciences can be tested in actuality and everyone has a freedom to do that. This is the reason that authenticity and universality of science has been accepted to be beyond suspicion. Anyone who needed science has used it also to his advantage.

In comparison, the first major difficulty with spirituality is that its hypotheses cannot be verified in physical terms. Whatever it talks about is invisible, sublime and often esoteric; facts and visible evidences or proofs perceptible by other sensory organs or instruments cannot be used to validate or establish its concepts. The second problem has been that different religious schools and philosophies have not stated spiritual concepts in the same form. There are large variations in their expositions. In some places their statements are even highly conflicting. This mutual conflict and differences give rise to doubts like, when all statements of science are so similar, why should there be so much discrepancy in the statements of spirituality? Either, only one of these is right or all of them are wrong. The facts that statements of spirituality cannot be proven in the laboratories, and that different sects present different and sometimes mutually contradicting theories, are the two main reasons why spirituality has never earned as much acceptance as the material-based science. In this intellectual era spirituality has not just been ignored, it has also been looked at with skepticism and even ridiculed.

Consciousness is superior to matter. Only a living being uses matter as per his will. This establishes the superiority of consciousness and hence of spirituality. Scientists decipher the knowledge of matter, energy and manifested Nature, and are seen to reap rich benefits by harnessing its potential. Then should not spiritual scientists be as successful and advanced in their own domain? However what is normally seen is exactly to the contrary. Spiritualists are seen riding on flights of fantasy; they talk about a lot of occult or magical powers based upon mythological stories but can never actually demonstrate any of it. How can inner peace and possibilities like ascent to heaven be called as authentic facts? Why should not these be rejected as falsehood based upon asinine beliefs?

These are such confusing matters that people today accept only the physically verifiable aspects of science, while the science of spirituality hangs around by the weak threads of faith and emotions. No one has any objections to molding gold in fire or testing its purity hundreds of times on a benchmark; why should spirituality then remain tied up within the confines of illusory or fictitious claims? Why shouldn't it put forth its principals in such a way that no one would try to challenge or falsify them? Those people who make a big propaganda about spirituality should at least not have been in a poor and downtrodden state. They should have influenced society to some extent and contributed to its development with their specialty. At least their surroundings and the environment around them should have been such that it could be said without doubt that there is no difference between what they speak and what they do.

Is Spirituality a Bane?

Modern scientists earn respect, praise, high position, wealth etc. Their contributions are recognized globally, appreciated by the masses and are remembered long afterwards. If spirituality is superior then the achievements of those who dedicate their efforts in this field should have been higher and not lesser. But this is not what is commonly observed. India has about six million so-called spiritual men in the attire of *sadhus* and *swamis*. Brahmins who have made religion as their means of livelihood are another about six million. So spiritual men and Brahmins add up to a population of about twelve million. This means that among every fifty people in India there is one person who earns his livelihood through religion or spirituality. If this ratio is taken with respect to only the Hindu population, the proportion of such persons would be more than double. In every 20-30 Hindus there is one spiritual man or woman, a *sadhu-sanyasi*, or a priest, or a preacher or a Brahmin. The personal state of all these spiritualists should have been relatively superior, but in reality most of them barely manage to make their ends meet and are normally seen propagating only misconceptions. If their state of affairs is analyzed, it can be clearly seen that they are much inferior in terms of health, education, character, talent and usefulness to society, compared to normal people.

There are about seven hundred thousands villages in our country. If the six million spiritual men who spend their lives in the name of religion are divided by the number of villages, it comes to about eight and a half 'spiritual persons' per village, whose expense are borne by the masses. Even if this large community is unaware of scientific methods or procedures of spirituality, it could still play an important role by taking up social work and contribute to society's development. It could take up simple activities like adult education, tree plantation, building gymnasiums, maintaining cleanliness, enhancing cooperation and rooting out superstitious practices, insane customs and social evils etc. With these activities alone there could have been a complete turn around in our country's intellectual, moral, and social state. But again the results in this regard are very disappointing. Such admirable saintly men who readily take up activities of service and contribute to the progress of our country, religion, society and culture can be counted on one's fingers.

The most popular religious activities among the Indian masses include pilgrimages, attending religious fairs, taking holy baths, visiting temples, singing *bhajan* and *kīrtan* (devotional songs), distributing free food and many other similar expensive pursuits. If the huge community of people that wastes its resources on such activities had understood the shabby and disorganized state of affairs of our nation and had worked on corrective measures, the situation would have been very different from what it is today. On the contrary, consumption of intoxicating drugs like opium, cocaine, tobacco etc, in the name of *'tantra'* and 'occult experiences', and promotion of blind faith under the shadow of distorted interpretation of religious texts are the only activities that seem to have been encouraged by the fake 'gurus' in this field.

A wide difference can thus be seen in the actions and accomplishments of modern scientists and spiritualists. Accordingly, superiority and inferiority of the two is ascribed. It is very unfortunate that the glory of spirituality falls much short in front of the might of scientific developments today. The value of a human being is evaluated on the basis of his achievements alone. On a weighing scale, the scientists' side turns out to be definitely heavier than the spiritualists. Conclusions can be easily drawn by this simple analysis. Only the naïve can be duped into basking in false glory, intellectual beings can be convinced only by hard facts. When huge financial resources are seen being wasted to support livelihood and ostensible behaviors of such a huge group of counter-productive people, feelings of disappointment, anger, disapproval and condemnation would naturally rise among the rational thinkers. They cannot be satisfied just by high-flown language and illusory mythology.

Grandeur of Spirituality:

So is this all that spirituality is? The answer to this is a clear and definite 'No'. Because, if we turn back the pages of history and analyze the ancient era, we can see that glorious ascent of spirituality has always bestowed pristine joy, rejuvenating calmness and illuminating inspiration. The radiance of spiritual personality is precious like the divine beauty of the Himalayas. There were very few *rishis* (spiritual sages) in the Vedic times, but the dignity of their personality, the grandeur of their *sādhanā* and the nobility of their service to humanity was so profound that even today its remembrance fills us with pride and reverence.

These spiritual scientists of yore used their own bodies and minds as laboratories. Through unflinching efforts and experimentation on the power of consciousness they had deciphered the hidden forces of Nature, and vital spiritual energy (*prāṇa*) indwelling within and outside their being. They had enriched their personalities with innumerable distinct qualities and preeminent talents. They had awakened the extrasensory faculties using sublime currents of consciousness-force, and acquired amazing supernatural powers.

By endeavoring ascetic fervors and penance for self-refinement, these ascetics used to shine like chiseled gold and used to prove their value to the society by their altruistic, sagacious deeds. They created several compositions on philosophies of real nature of the world, and on yogic and spiritual experiments on mind-body system and the inner self. Their lives were exemplars of foremost signs of spirituality, namely, beatifying love and sensitivity for all beings. Such was the influence of their spiritual aura that in their hermitages, lions and cows would share a common source of drinking water. Whoever visited them and lived in their abode would return with an illumined outlook and improved personality. Their proximity was like that of a touchstone, and their patronage and blessings could fulfill all wishes. They always lived in bliss and radiated the same all around. The peerless roles they played in solving the problems of man and society deserve high praise.

This is not the right place for singing paeans of great *rishis*. However there are innumerable contributions made by them that can be called as extraordinary by all means: like Vyas's Literature, Jamadagni's hermitage-school, Nagarjuna's Chemistry, Charak's Botany, Sushrut's Surgery, Yagyavalkya's research on *Yagya*, Maitreyi's sacrifice for attaining true knowledge, Vishwamitra's Science of Mantras, Parashuram's fight for uprooting injustice and vices, Vashishtha's efforts to re-establish *Satyuga* in the *Tretayuga* through Ram, Dronacharya's skill of Archery, Dadhichi's donation of his bones for the construction of *vajra*, Bhagirath's devout ascetic endeavor (*tapa*) to invoke the flow of the holy Ganges, Anusuya's *tapa* to invite the water currents of Mandakini, Panini's Sanskrit Grammar, Patanjali's Yoga, Vaiseshik's Atomic Science, Daksha's Physics, Arjun's mastery in battles, Agastya's capacity of drinking ocean, Narad's travails across the world for people's welfare, Vishwakarma's Architecture, Kaundinya's efforts of global dissemination of Indian Culture, Chanakya's establishment of university and so on. *Rishis* like Suta and Shaunak used to organize discussions on religion at different places. So strong was the spiritual strength of the *rishis* that they transformed the lives of evil men like Valmiki and Angulimal and uplifted them to high portals. Noble contributions of the *rishi* culture continued in the post Vedic ages as well. Buddha's renaissance of religion and Shankaracharya's dissemination of divine knowledge changed the trends of their times in the righteous direction. The *rishis* of medieval and later times made possible the much needed social reformation and revival of human values against the tides of cultural decline, and political anarchy. Samarth Ramdas made a plan for struggle for freedom and national integrity and got it executed through his disciples — great kings like Pratap, Shivaji and Chhatrasal. All credit for Chandragupta's successes is due to Chanakya. Great saints like Kabir, Raidas and Meerabai, removed the caste disparity in the society. Vivekanand the disciple of Ramkrishna Paramhans placed the shaky edifice of Indian Culture onto a firm footing. Swami Dayanand the disciple of Virjanand waged a battle and destroyed widespread ostentations propounded in the name of religion. Such were these truly spiritual persons that simply remembering their personalities and great deeds itself is enough to spark an elevating thrill.

They molded the character and guided the noble deeds of great Kings and Queens like Harshwardhan, Ahilyabai, Ashok, Karna, Harishchandra, Ashwapati, Chakravarti Bharat etc, who created glorifying annals of the Indian History. Their protection and guidance inspired divinity in the great women like Savitri, Sukanya, Kunti, Gandhari, Renuka, Arundhati and so on. Under whose mentorship young princes like Dhruv, Prahlad, Luv-Kush, Abhimanyu etc could attain high realms of immortal distinction, even the cows of whose Ashrams were so special that the mighty Kings like Dileep went there to look after them – take them for gazing; grand empires were bent on whose feet, whose curses ruined the devilish might and uprooted the wrongs in no time, whose blessings were like divine boons, such was the majesty of the *rishis* – the scientists of spirituality. Their field by no means can be termed ordinary, to enter which the likes of Vishawamitra and Bhatruhari even abdicated their gigantic kingdoms. The science that transmutes ordinary mortal beings into angelic paragons cannot be a maze of illusion.

It was because of their preeminent talents that India used to be called the Guru of the World. Their adept guidance had enlightened the masses to the extent that the thirty-three crore (330 million) citizens of India in the Satayuga were counted as *devatās*. These examples illustrate the miraculous achievements of the *rishis* by adopting the principles of spirituality. Their presence alone had brought enormous good fortunes to India; they had nurtured this land into what may be referred as 'superior to the heavens'.

All human beings are alike, but among the scores of ordinary beings, rise of a few to extraordinary levels proves that whoever attained greatness must have had some strong support. This support is nothing but the light of spirituality that bestows glory and status of a divine being to this mortal structure of bones and flesh called human being. This is not a hypothesis or a mere statement; the lives of true achievers of spirituality indeed prove it.

It is clear then that the science of the soul is great in itself and its capability and dignity is no less than that of any other branch of science. In fact it is greater. However, when people do not garner requisite resources to search for the real diamond, and merely satisfy their desire by acquiring pieces of glass, then they are denied the vaunted glory. Nowadays people wish to achieve all the payback by pursuing namesake prayers, rituals and remembrance of God's names, which actually is achievable only by adopting spirituality in true sense. The seekers as well as critics of the science of spirituality should note that no one can become a spiritualist by renouncing home, living on alms and dyeing one's clothes in saffron. The only way is to inculcate spiritual ideals into every aspect of one's life, every action, every fragment of one's body, and into each wave of thought. The principle of right achievement at a right price applies everywhere. Those who get waylaid from this only earn exhaustion, disappointment, failure and ridicule.

An Insight into
True Spirituality | 2

Those who enter the realm of spirituality must first read its alphabet and understand on what basis does the supreme consciousness descend upon a human being to enrich him with extraordinary powers, how does he become capable of performing amazing deeds, and how does he transform himself to an enlightened person endowed with chiseled personality and superlative talents.

The Basis of Spiritual Progress:

The Supreme Consciousness-Force (*Parabraham*) is Omnipresent. Its evolutionary power pervades the entire universe. All the processes of Nature are governed by the system of laws of this Absolute Force. This eternal power (*śakti*) neither favors nor discriminates against anyone. Unlike a human being's mind, the supreme power does not distinguish between self and others. It neither needs anyone's acts of pleasing nor gifts and presents. One who is just and impartial simply cannot have affection for anyone based upon acts like repeated chanting of His names and offerings of flowers, rice grains, and what not!

God's favors shower down for special reasons and accumulate where they are supposed to. After a warm summer when the land and water get warmed up, the rainy season appears to create a balance. Rains fall everywhere, but the water gets collected only in a catchment area, pond, or where there is substantial depth. Water does not get collected on rocks despite falling upon them.

To attach oneself to the Supreme Soul and to attract His powers, favors and supramental talents one needs to develop an appropriate 'personal magnetism'. A magnet either attracts pieces of iron around it, or itself gets pulled towards a larger magnet. Supreme Soul is like a big magnet. By being pulled towards Him we can gather within us all the virtuous qualities that He has.

It rains a lot at places where the tree cover is thick. The attraction of trees pulls down the rain clouds and forces them to shed rain. The water that falls gets collected where there is depth. Rivers, drains, lakes contain water only because they have depth. We need to inculcate deserving qualities within us so that we become worthy of the favors of the Supreme Soul, and the support and respect from the people and society.

Human body is a treasure chest full of magic. In each and every bit of it lies a repository of amazing powers. All the profound activities that go on in the solar system at a grand scale also go on within a tiny atom. The only difference is that this grandeur lies concealed in a dormant and invisible state, like a seed. If his capabilities could be awakened in the righteous manner then a human being, who seems to be an insignificant living object, can become a visible representative of the sublime Consciousness-Force that pervades the cosmic expansion. Till now, the functioning of only 7 percent of the brain has been understood. The functioning of the remaining 93 percent, which is said to be the seat of subconscious and superconscious faculties, still remains unknown. Of all the bio-electric current that flows through nerves of the body, a very small fraction gets used-up to maintain body systems while some of it is also spent in thinking and contemplating. Its most evolved component, which exists within us as the highly potent vital spiritual energy (*prāṇa*), remains completely unused. If the immense potential of this *prāṇa* could be awakened, expanded and put into action, then with this alone an ordinary looking person can become extraordinary and elevate himself to be placed on the pedestal of great souls, *rishi*s or divine beings. It is entirely up to him to achieve this success.

Methods of Spirituality: *Tapa* and *Yoga*

Capabilities of a human being remain subdued due to his faults and vices, the weaknesses, blemishes and inferior quality of his character, due to his sins and misdeeds, and his evil tendencies and corrupt thinking. The first step in spirituality is to wage a battle against all this filth and immorality and to defeat it. This process of cleansing and rectification is called *tapa* (penance). *Tapa* literally means – to heat up. In the field of spirituality the process of 'heating up' refers to searching out with sharp acumen all the unworthiness from the external and the internal persona, to put in intense efforts to set right the attitudes and tendencies linked with them and then to reorient the mind with ascetic disciplines and firm determination. It is easier to fight against enemies that are outside because they can be seen with eye and can be attacked and defended against by several means. But how does one fight with oneself? Evil tendencies and untoward thinking, becoming a part of one's nature, enter into practice, and then turning into habits and intrinsic impressions, hide within one's personality with such subtlety that it becomes very hard to even recognize them. Only one with a penetrating introspective sight can search them out and designate them as his enemies instead of habitual friends. The strategies to uproot them can be made only afterwards.

As described in the holy Gita, when Arjun made excuses on the battlefront of Mahabharata, Lord Krishna prepared him to fight for the righteous cause. The spiritual explanation of this entire episode and the preachings of Lord Krishna is to prepare oneself to fight with unflinching valor against the unworthiness that has been with us for a long time and has got united with us like a close friend or a family member. This Herculean battle is *tapa*. It is not simply putting the body to extreme physical ardor and pain (as is commonly understood). When a washer man cleans clothes he first boils them up, then applies soap and then hits and beats them clean. In *tapa* one needs to carry out all these acts upon himself – upon the physical and mental body and the inner self. All those who have done *tapa* have had to apply the same process and strategy.

There are four main components of *tapa*: (i) continence over the senses; (ii) orderliness and efficient management of time; (iii) control over financial expenses; and, (iv) restraining and constructive channelizing of the thought process. Our life is divided and distributed within these four facets only. Desires and actions of the sense organs, availability and use of time, worldly resources and mental faculties define our life in general. Therefore, in trying to implement the refinement and adept regulation associated with these four, practically all aspects of life get covered. This cleansing in a sense, leads to purification and rectification of one's entire course of life. One has to say a clear and definite 'no' to the untoward attractions and temptations of the mind. And just saying 'no' is not enough; one needs to actually accept farsighted discerning intelligence as his guide and then has to train his old personality to compulsorily follow its diktat.

The second step forward for self-refinement, improvement and enhancement of worthiness is called *'yoga'*. The literary meaning of *yoga* is 'to connect' or 'to unite'. But unite what with what? *Yoga* means uniting the self with the Supreme Soul, the *Parabrahm*. The only method to achieve this is, to begin with, inculcation of greatness associated with human dignity into character, behavior and day-to-day activities. Man's personal God is nothing but an absolute assemblage of righteous tendencies and virtues. God's all-encompassing form is simply incomprehensible to any human being. Instead of attempting to imagine the infinite reality of God or to realize Him in sublime realms, it is more appropriate for us to visualize Him in every thing existing in the cosmic expansion (*Virāṭa Brahm*), to see His manifestation in the world we live in (*Viśwa Brahm*), and to experience Him in every pulse of life (*Jīvana Brahm*).

Our lives could be linked (have *yoga*) with this form of God alone. In short, this *yoga* means, elevating our notion of self, cultivating and expanding righteous tendencies, altruistic attitude and divine attributes in our own lives. In this regard, the concepts of Vedanta Philosophy clarify the meaning of *yoga* in totality. *Soham*! *Śivoham*! *Satchidānandoham*! *Tat-twam-asi*! *Ayam Ātmā Brahm*! The secret underlying these words is that man's interior and exterior must be divine (like his ultimate reality).

So the spiritual endeavors of *sādhanā* or the process that eventually transforms human being to Supreme Being, an atom to the cosmic expansion, has two aspects, first *tapa* and second *yoga*. *Tapa* means to root out evil tendencies and *yoga* means to instill and foster righteous tendencies and noble qualities. It should be understood that the more one assimilates superiority in thoughts, righteousness in character and nobility in his conduct, the more rapidly he progresses towards self-refinement and self-evolution.

Before dyeing, clothes need to be washed thoroughly. Before seeds are sown, the ground needs to be cleared and thoroughly ploughed. Before walls are built, grounds need to be dug deep to lay the foundations. Before placing images of God and offering prayers to Him, the place and the equipments to be used need to be sanctified. *Tapa* is for cleansing and *yoga* is for refining and elevating. One who succeeds and proves himself in these two steps, can be understood to have consolidated his path. His preparations are completed in proportion to his dedication and progress in *sādhanā*, to reach his ultimate goal of spirituality.

A mother loves her child more than herself. She devotes all her time in taking care of the child and supporting him. But when he spoils his clothes with faeces and gets dirty all over, then despite the child's crying and urging, the mother does not take him in her lap nor feeds him milk. Her first attention is towards changing the soiled or dirty clothes and washing and bathing the child. Only after the child is cleansed up, he is taken in the lap and breast-fed. God also follows the same principle. He keeps His distance and remains aloof from humans till the process of self-refinement is complete. Negligence in this regard is the main reason why one remains untouched by the divine grace of God. Self-purification is the first and the most important step on the ladder of spirituality. Once this phase is over, the process of self-transformation and spiritual enlightenment begins at a brisk pace.

Those who prove themselves in examinations and competitions earn promotion. If the performance is extraordinary, awards are also granted. For a job appointment to a high post all the candidates are made to undergo tough tests. Those who prove themselves worthy get the appointment. At the job as well their skill is continuously evaluated and accordingly the chances of promotion are given. The rule says that this process must go on without any partiality. In public life this rule may get transgressed at times but in the supreme royal court of God, this rule is an absolute incontrovertible principle. So rather than pleading and coaxing a deity, it is much more appropriate for a seeker of spirituality to try hard and make devout efforts to inculcate good qualities and righteousness. One must keep proving one's worthiness again and again like pure gold does each time it is tested in fire or on a touchstone. On this basis alone can a man's worth be evaluated in this world and in the court of the Supreme Eternal

Power. On this basis alone one receives divine favors. This is a well-defined 'highway' to attain supreme talents and superhuman potentials. Those who follow indefinite shortcuts instead unnecessarily lose their way and get entangled in thorny webs and mires. The result of their endeavours is only fatigue, disappointment and failure.

Misconceptions in Spirituality:

So many superstitions abound in this world. So many insane social customs, convictions and even common habits prevalent in the society illustrate that superstitions are firmly rooted like addictions and intrinsic tendencies. There is no basis behind discriminating between boys and girls. The common beliefs of superiority and inferiority of castes also do not hold ground. Who ever gained anything from intoxication? Belief in auspicious and inauspicious times entangles one into so many doubts and uncertainties. Even then people have been believing in all these superstitions for so long. Intellectual illusions are no less rampant; at least half the world has been duped into believing these.

A similar misconception is that God can be enticed by first chanting His name and following religious rituals, and then can be tricked into fulfilling our reasonable or unreasonable desires. This is imposing a big accusation on the glory of the Almighty, and tarnishing God's discerning intelligence and love for justice. In medieval times, local lords would be enthralled by listening to the praise offered by sycophants and would shower expensive gifts upon them. If we consider God to be at par with such men and attempt to lure Him by obsequiousness and sycophancy, then surely we have failed to understand the greatness of God. If we try to become His favorite by 'bribing' Him with food, rich clothing, golden parasols etc and then try to get Him to fulfill all our unreasonable demands, then this is nothing less than demeaning Him. With these despicable means when even in the real world it is not possible to trick a bank manager into parting with money, or trick an inspector into corrupt practice, or lure a judge, or acquire a dignified post without suitable qualifications, then on what basis can one expect that God – the Omniscient would fall prey to these cheap tricks? He is not so naïve that He, like a bird or a fish, can be lured into traps by baits and then used to earn unfair profits.

The only purpose behind *sādhanā* and *upāsanā* is self-cleansing and self-progress. In one word it is enhancing one's worthiness. It has been said that *tapa* is rooting out evil tendencies and *yoga* is fostering righteousness. Whoever adopts these fundamental principles with determination and sincerity enhances his worthiness and so becomes very dear to God. Instead, by adopting wily means and terming them as devotion one can never be dear to God nor can one become fit to receive any of His splendid glory.

The main purpose behind practices like chanting of names, meditation, worship, collective prayers, religious ceremonies etc also is that through these we cultivate and imbibe the virtues like benevolence and righteousness within ourselves. By understanding the secret and the hidden indications behind these practices, we need to take up activities that are dear to the Ruler of the Universe.

It is said that human birth is one that is attained with great effort. It is the most artistic and preeminent creation of the Supreme Creator. Human birth is entrusted to a soul with an expectation and anticipation that it would evolve from individual incompleteness into completeness and at the same time would dedicate itself to contribute in advancing and shaping of this world into a better and happier place through persistent effort and service. By adopting this farsighted prudence into personal life alone can one become a true devotee of God. Through the *sādhanā* of self-transformation, auspicious gains (*puṇya*) are earned in the form of virtuous potentials. And through the *sādhanā* of altruistic service, the true benefit of religiousness is acquired in the form of rejuvenating peace. These two together fulfill the requirement that results in attaining the glory and dignity of a meaningful life.

If one can steer out of all the cobwebs of illusions and superstitions that abound the field of spirituality and understand its true nature and its methods, then the outcome would be definitely what has been described in the scriptures by great seers and sung by great saints.

On the
Touchstone of Reality | 3

The first principle of science is that any concept should be taken to be true only when the outcomes as predicted by it can actually be attained. Every one accepts a fact when it is demonstrated to be true in real. Therefore science is accepted by all. The science of spirituality has lagged behind in this and as a result has been subjected to disregard and disrespect.

Loss of Faith:

Most of those who attempt to follow spirituality can be heard saying that despite following religious practices for a long time nothing much has been achieved, all their time and effort has got wasted, that the whole exercise has been futile and the results have been disappointing.

People usually start with high expectations, but put in only superficial efforts to garner requisite resources to achieve what they want. So the results they obtain are nowhere close to their expectations. Faulty planning, or flawed implementation of the plans are the prominent reason that results may not be as desired. Falling off after climbing great heights risks grave injuries. Similar is the state when listening to great narratives the expectations are raised high, but nothing is actually attained.

Several people wish to realize God, and wish that all their lofty desires would be fulfilled in a moment by divine grace. For this they take up some religious practices as well. However when the desired results are not attained neither do they try to find faults within themselves, nor do they put in efforts to find mistakes in the methods they followed. Instead the basic principle itself is said to be wrong or deceitful. When there is none to explain or reply back it becomes even easier to blame anyone for anything. Thus 'poor' spirituality gets all the blame and ends up being mistaken as obscure imagination, whim of emotional excitation or mythological allegory. The scarcity of original ancient texts since the medieval times and misinterpretations by some selfish minds had added to such misconceptions in the later periods of civilization. So with passage of time intellectuals began to deny the whole concept of spirituality itself.

Waning of Spirituality in Modern Times:

In its infancy and early days of exuberance material science forcefully proclaimed that there is no such thing as God and the self-governing cycle of nature is the one that maintains all the operations. The existence of soul was denied similarly. It was claimed that a human being is nothing more than a tree that moves about. With time it withers and dies. There is no such thing as the world beyond. The capable can keep exploiting the incapables so that in this world the ugliness of incapability can be kept under check. When consciousness itself has no independent identity and only activities in the brain govern and control the limbs and organs, then the science of consciousness and the knowledge of spirituality can have no existence. In such a situation then, it is futile to expect any kind of good results from spirituality.

Whatever materialism proclaimed in its infirm, infantile voice, immature people accepted as the ultimate truth without verifying, studying or researching. A new *mullā* (Islamic priest) at a mosque in his excitement cries out louder than the rest; in a similar way the pseudo scientists or the so-called rational thinkers of that period began to support and spread atheism in a frenetic voice.

On the other side, the field of spirituality was filled with self-contended philosophers having only bookish knowledge. They never understood the necessity of inner realization, deeper thinking, logical arguments, facts, proofs and examples. They accepted the words of the scriptures as the whole truth. For them each word spoken by whomever they regarded a great man itself established its correctness. So they kept on presenting their thoughts through scriptures and other hearsay stories. They were not prepared to formulate a battle plan against atheism in accordance with the changing times when intellectualism and realism were steadily gaining acceptance. They did not understand that an argument needs to be contradicted with another argument, a fact with another fact, a proof with another proof, and an example with another example. These so-called spiritual men had no clue about principles of science since they never read science. The situation was like coming together of a deaf and a dumb. Science never tried to investigate the truth hidden in the depths of spirituality, and spirituality never felt the need or never found the time to understand the philosophy of science. The outcome was that spirituality had to accept defeat against science. The words of atheist philosophers like Nietzsche, Marx and Russell earned a lot of respect and fame and the second front of these philosophers waned out the light of spirituality and subdued its strength.

The third aspect has already been touched upon previously that people used to try to inveigle God into fulfilling their selfish desires but to no avail. They wanted to physically see God to divest Him of His powers. But the all-encompassing power that God is, has to be formless, how could it assume a form? How could it communicate and interact with a human like another? But hearsay narratives and blind faith kept encouraging them and they kept on hoping that once they would see God it would be easy to hold Him captive and get all their works done. Such a thing never worked out and their desires were never met. Attaining magical and supernatural powers and then milking the faith of masses by conjuring them was also a complicated task which could be carried out only by clever, magician like people. These days such conjurers alone have been elevated to the status of so-called God-men. Before their trickery and deceit is laid bare they wind up their shops and put them up elsewhere.

These three aforementioned reasons alone are mainly responsible for wavering people's, and more specifically, intellectuals' faith in spirituality. These compel them to stay away from spirituality. Only the limited segment of traditionalists, superstitious and God-fearing men now supports the entire structure of spirituality like an irony. Often one sees that spirituality has degenerated to all sorts of improper activities carried out by narrow-minded religious communities.

An analysis of the current state tends one to conclude that day-by-day the side of spirituality is growing weaker. Prudence would steadily part its ways with spirituality. No structure can stand upon the base of superstitions, it has to collapse tomorrow or the day after. How long can a wall of sand grains stand its grounds? For how long can magicians keep milking God-fearing men as their profession? The future looks completely bleak when one looks at this side alone.

Sight of Resurrection of Spiritual Glory:

However, a ray of hope has shone from the horizon in a new form. It has assured that truth has the strength of thousands of elephants. It can never die. Even if the entire world rises in opposition, it can stay up on its feet. Consciousness-force is not unreal. When by toying around with inanimate matter such repositories of capabilities and piles of conveniences can be created, then it cannot be that dealings with the consciousness-force would be completely useless. The potential of soul is not so inferior that it can be ignored or put to ridicule by hues and cries raised by some immature, excitable men.

The everlasting principles of spirituality had propagated in the early centuries based upon peoples' faith in them. The whole setup of spirituality worked fine in an organized way then. But as the times changed the thinking class began to value intellectualism, practicality and material science more. So now it was necessary that the basis of faith be proven on the touchstone of reality. Times demanded that if spirituality had to stay alive and remain respected, then it had to go through the fire-test of practicality and had to prove its worth just like Sita, who had to prove her piety after returning from Lanka by entering and emerging unscathed from fire.

Several small steps were taken by some saintly savants in this direction from various platforms but no comprehensive programme ever emerged. Saint Vinoba also had said once that spirituality and science must join hands, but he also could not go into the nuances of how that would happen or who would do that. Several enlightened reformers all over the world have been expressing the need for the same, but their thought process also could not take the next step of formulating an outline for the task. Eminent *siddha* of Gayatri, distinguished scholar and writer and social reformer, Pandit Shriram Sharma Acharya pioneered the renaissance of spirituality in new scientific light, in the most practical way with the purpose of mass-elevation.

The balancing power of the creator seems to have now created models to fulfill this demand of the times while holding its threads in His own very hands. Brahmavarchas Research Centre, Haridwar, founded by Pandit Shriram Sharma Acharya, is the foremost institute, which is steadfastly working towards integration of modern and ancient sciences and spirituality. Its resolution is – firmly establishing the eternal principles of spirituality by harmonizing the accepted principles of material science with them.

Earlier it was thought that both these streams flow in different directions. One stream considers as true only what is perceivable, while the other what is beyond. Material science can express itself through senses or through instruments, but consciousness is subtle and expresses itself through thoughts, feelings and experiences. So is it ever possible to resolve this divergence? Such doubts and misgivings were proved to be baseless. New paths were created and new processes were formulated based on which in the coming days the very atheists would first get converted into staunch believers. Material science is based upon facts, and when facts would support the tenets of spirituality then in its honesty science would have to accept all that it had denied in the past. True science is never obstinate and fixated. Whatever Newton thought and said is in contradiction with the accepted concepts of today, but stubbornness did not come in the way to create obstructions. Unlike communalism, it was never proclaimed from the platform of science that 'we are right and others are wrong'. Prudence always accepts the principle of 'whatever is true is ours' and not 'whatever is ours is the truth'. On this basis science has always progressed with an open-ended approach by correcting its past mistakes and in future too efforts would continue to search for the true reality further.

Brahmavarchas Research Centre has supervised many laboratory experiments and research projects to scientifically establish several principles of spirituality and to demonstrate their benefits in overall wellbeing of mankind in the present times. Most importantly, it has shown spirituality as an evolved science of psychological and intellectual elevation and chiseled refinement of personality. Outcome of this research is periodically published in Akhand Jyoti, Yug Shakti Gayatri magazines, a journal published by the Dev Sanskriti University, Haridwar. Some recent research results (parts of some PhD theses) are also published in reputed international science journals. A series of books is also being written. There is a strong desire to further expand and enhance the scope of research in the coming days, after the initial work is completed. There is also a plan to regularly publish a bulletin.

Acceptance of People:

As spirituality pertains to human being and not merely to some inert elements of Nature, in addition to the theoretical and laboratory research, there was also a need to prove elementary concepts by applying them on people. When a new medicine is invented, it does not get approval for general use just because good chemicals have been used in its manufacture. First it is tested upon small animals and then upon humans. Only when the benefits of the new medicine are well established that it gets approval. Any concept is accepted these days only when it can convince all, so the need to convince people cannot be bypassed.

One major hurdle in conducting spiritual experiments on people is that it is very difficult to get such people who are willing to accept and thoroughly adopt the prime principles of spirituality. Spirituality stands for a complete redefinition of the way of living. Most only want quick fix remedies, while self-cleansing is a very challenging task. And then the requirement that all the achievements must be utilized not for selfish interests but for the betterment of the whole world with selflessness, is tougher to meet. General tendency among masses today is to make easy profit, like winning millions of rupees by investing just one rupee in lottery.

But in such circumstances how can the desire to buy off the invaluable at a cheap price be fulfilled? How can a sword made of wood conquer challenging battles? How can the mere child-play of religious rituals and superficial spiritual practices reap rich awards that match up with achievements of those who earned respect through arduous endeavors? A solution has been found to this problem as well. A huge group of millions of men and women has been entrusted the responsibility to demonstrate the practicality of spirituality. After all, a work is honored and appreciated only when it is concluded with strong supporting evidences. We shall read more about this group of people and Brahmavarchas Research Institute in Chapter 7.

Enrich Entire Life with Spirituality | 4

People have several misconceptions regarding God's true nature and form. But there are many more delusions regarding the objectives and methods of *sādhanā*, the spiritual levels of *sādhaks* and gurus and so on. This chapter clarifies some of these misconceptions and explains the basic tenets of spirituality. It also explains the reasons behind unusual attires and acts of the spiritual men and how in modern times people have misinterpreted and confused spirituality with these externalities and forgotten the true spirit of spirituality.

God as Formless and as Incarnated:

According to Upanishads the reflection of the eternal consciousness force (*Brahm*) lies in the inner cores of heart and appears like a glow of a flame of the size of a thumb. This is a thought for contemplation and experience. In an introspective state of deep meditation if such feelings are cultivated, the process of self-realization gets going more smoothly. The way to realize God as the formless is to nurture the feeling that God lives within our beings and His home, this body of ours, must be kept holy and sanctified like a sacred shrine; we must learn to be self-reliant, and continuously strive for self-purification. This is the root of all *sādhanās* of experiencing the formless *Brahm*.

On the other hand some scriptures mention of Arjun, Yashoda, Kaushalya, Kakbhushundi as having seen God in the incarnated form. Accepting the inner urge and prayers of these pure souls, God revealed before them, His manifested being that encompassed everything in this entire cosmic expanse and enlightened them to perform *sādhanā* of this form by devoting themselves to the service of society and inculcation and dissemination of righteousness.

The main purpose behind religious practices and rituals is also the same – to awaken and evolve the consciousness within us through these. The concept behind chanting names of God and meditation is to remind us of God who has given us this life, His heritage(?) and His expectations from us, and accordingly chart out an illustrious plan for our lives. The use of sandalwood in prayers reminds us to cultivate and develop the environment around us. Offering rice grains reminds us to offer our resources for the upliftment of the society. The lamp reminds us to imbibe within us the radiance of divine knowledge and motivates us to contribute to the development of society. This holistic way of thinking and living alone can please God.

The Soul of Sādhanā:

Faith is prime in *sādhanā*. Ramayan says that faith and belief represent Gods Parvati and Shiva and every devotee has to first take their refuge. Only then the perfect foundation is laid for attaining divine talents and powers. Meera's Krishna, Ramkrishna Paramhans' Kali and Eklavya's mud statute of Dronacharya are proofs that by instilling faith any medium can become the basis for acquiring divine powers. On this basis alone a stone or sculpture gets enshrined as an idol of a deity or an image of God; in the absence of faith it would remain simply a stone. The same applies to chanting too, if one has devotional faith, a configuration of words may become a *mantra*, otherwise a mere combination of syllables. The immense potential that a divine form or a *mantra* has, is in fact nothing else but an expression of intensity of the *sādhak*'s faith. One's god-form is a reflection of one's inner imagination, echo of one's intrinsic thoughts. So though it is true that God has created man, but it is also not incorrect that man also has cast God into a form. No other living being can experience the presence of God.

An arrow becomes a potent and deadly weapon only when the string of the bow that launches it, is mounted and stretched properly. Else that sharp arrow can create only a small wound when pressed against skin. Likewise, the character and personality of a *sādhak* alone make his *sādhanā* powerful. If these are impure and weak, nothing would be achieved by chanting or religious practices. A sinful man like Valmiki turned into a great saint by adopting a virtuous life and shunning his evil deeds even though he repeated the name of Lord Ram in reverse, while Queen Kaikeyi and her maid Manthara lived with Ram Himself but earned only ill fame. The saying *"Rāma Se Baḍā Rāma Kā Nāma"* also implies that devotional chanting of His name through pure heart is more powerful than the human-incarnation of god Ram. It is this force of (faith in) His name that inspires the likes of Gandhi and transforms them into Mahatma – great beings.

An Adept Guru:

A lot of importance has been given to blessings and guidance of a guru (a noble master) for spiritual upliftment. Guru is placed higher than God Himself. Many people seek enlightened men who can take them across to God. However they forget that only a wooden boat can float on river, a piece of stone would sink immediately. In this world there is no dearth of capable Gurus who themselves constantly search for deserving disciples to pass on their knowledge to. But why would they ever pass on their hard earned earnings to unworthy men for wrong use? Such a favor would only enhance their pride and result in their destruction. Several demons like Ravan, Kumbhakaran, Marich, Hiranyakashyapu, Vruttasur, Bhasmasur, Mahishasur etc attained great boons after severe ascetic endeavors, but the final result was only their ruin.

A father of a worthy grown-up daughter searches far and wide for a deserving groom, and considers himself lucky when he gets one. If some unworthy man asks for the hand of his daughter, the father would severely reproof him. Accomplished gurus are also not so naïve that they cannot recognize a selfish and unworthy seeker and would give away their earnings, their *sādhanā*, just based on sycophancy. They accept a disciple only after substantial test of his/her purity, sincerity and devotion to the noble goal of spiritual ascent.

The Basic Tenets of Spirituality:

Evolution of the soul is always slow and gradual. It takes time and needs endurance coupled with persistent efforts. One must not lose his patience if it takes a few rebirths to cleanse up the evil *sanskārs* (intrinsic impressions in the inner self) accumulated over in the previous births traversing through '84 lakh *yonis'* (numerous life forms). It isn't right to rise up like a bubble and then settle down like foam. One must have persistence like Goddess Parvati who continued her *sādhanā* to win over Lord Shiva despite knowing that He has gone into a deep trance for a thousand years. When Saptarshi, the seven Vedic sages, went to examine her devotion and discouraged her from continuing her *sādhanā,* she calmly replied that even if she has to take millions of rebirths and lead austere lives as this one, she would prefer that; she would wed Lord Shiva only or else remain unmarried. True resources of a *sādhak* are patience, firm resolve and courage. One who has these would certainly attain his goal one day or the other. It is essential for every *sādhak*, every seeker of divine light, to understand and firmly assimilate these virtues. Note that impulsive people turn impatient, lose their heart and give up the chosen path. They can't accomplish any *sādhanā*.

Divine powers and supernormal talents (*siddhis*) are definitely attained by devout *sādhanā* but these are bestowed with the constraint that they ought to be used only to help and benefit others, and to spread benevolent tendencies in society. They ought not to be used for selfish means and to fulfill one's wishes and desires. The means to fulfill personal wishes should be rightfully earned using one's mental and physical efforts, and talents, while divine blessings and *sādhanā* of sages ought to be reserved for those who have dedicated themselves to uplift the society. These should not be wasted in providing comforts and luxuries to those who deceive by proclaiming themselves to be true disciples.

Sādhanā stands for infusing all round excellence into life. On one hand it means creation of an exemplary, praise-worthy and inspiring personality, while on the other it means generous dedication of one's efforts, time and resources to develop and beautify this world-garden. Those who walk this royal path quickly attain immense inner-satisfaction, and adulation and support from masses, in addition to divine affection from invisible worlds. This much is enough to make one feel that the purpose that he was bestowed life with, is met.

Those who are obsessed with amassing wealth or are engaged in sensual pleasures and those who are filled with self-praise and ego are in fact intoxicated beings. Higher powers do not bestow their blessings to such men as this would only further their intoxication and ignorance, and quicken their downfall. Why would they hang a stone around the neck of a drowning person and thus ensure his ruin. It is essential for people who tread the path of *sādhanā* to understand these basic principles.

While adopting the principles of spirituality there is no need to make accusations like this world is an illusion and we need to break free from the worldly ties. Nor there is a need to wander around and live on alms. Among the ideal saints in the modern times the principles of Mahatma Gandhi and

Vinoba ji are the most appropriate. Living normal lives but adopting principles of simple living and high thinking is sufficient. If the mind is not allowed to wander behind excessive greed, attachment and egoism, then meeting the basic requirements of a small family does not require much effort. If family members are trained to stand on their own feet and educated with morality then there would be no need to leave immense wealth behind for them. Life should be balanced in such a way that first half of it is spent on providing for the family and livelihood, and the later half is preserved for carrying out benevolent deeds and serving the society. In today's times the most appropriate and important act of service is refinement of people's way of thinking.

Each person who wishes to adopt spirituality must try to cast his life in the form of a true Brahmin. When the traditions of Brahminhood were alive a large section of people used to take up altruistic service as their duty, and through their good deeds the emotional as well as the social structure of not only our country but the entire world used to be enriched. India was once called Jagdguru, a beacon light for the whole world and its countless contributions to the world were widely appreciated. This was due to the services of this large group of people towards the development of society. The tradition of saints and Brahmins was responsible for creation of men with divine attributes. However, in present times, Brahminhood has got relegated to lineage and sainthood to just dressing up in saffron. The true characteristics and qualities of these have almost disappeared. As a result the thought processes and character of the entire humanity has got corrupted. Once evil tendencies pervaded the social ambience, several problems surfaced and disasters began to strike. The only way to tackle the present situation is by reviving the Age of Truth (*Satyuga*). This can be achieved by creating a new generation of true saints and Brahmins. This is possible only by inculcation of spirituality in each mind and heart. This would require refinement of thoughts and cultivation of sensitivity in emotions, attitude and actions. Every spiritually inclined individual, every seeker of religion must begin this process of evolution from himself.

To spiritualize one's life, one must plan to live first half of the life like a Brahmin, who strives for great values and knowledge, and the second half of the life like a saint who is dedicated to uplift the society. To begin with, in the first half of life days can be planned in such a way that out of twenty four hours, seven may go towards sleep, five hours towards fulfilling daily needs and chores, and eight hours towards earning livelihood and profession. This would add up to twenty hours and leave four hours for virtuous deeds. Of these one hour could be used for *sādhanā* and one for *swādhyāya* (self-study in the light of the thoughts of elevated souls) and the remaining two hours for meeting people and helping refinement and positive orientation of their thoughts and attitude. The second half of life must be completely devoted to altruistic service and ascent of society in the traditions of saints. This is what corresponds to adopting *Vānprastha*. If some finances are available they should be deposited in bank to live off on the interest. If not then the needs must be met through the support of dedicated charity organizations like Gayatri Pariwar. The method of collecting alms from homes might have been acceptable earlier, but that is not so today. Hence before adopting spiritual life one must plan ahead one's personal finances for respectful subsistence.

What Spirituality Is Not?

Having explained the basic and timeless tenets of spirituality it is now worthwhile to clarify some of the delusions that have engulfed this field and have reduced its worth and utility. What is seen in the name of spirituality today is an irony and just blind following of traditions. For example, in earlier days, ascetics living in forests would keep some smoke-fire lit nearby while carrying out their spiritual penance, to keep themselves warm in cold mountainous regions. Their smoke-fire would also help meet their requirements of cooking their simple food and keeping dangerous beasts at bay. Forests then used to be littered with dry fallen wood, and using this wood for fire would help in cleansing the area as well. In today's times, lighting and maintaining smoke-fire has become a worthless tradition but yet diligently followed in several so-called hermitages and spiritual centers. Today the wood is expensive and is obtained by destroying forest cover When the ascetics these days live in temperate regions, wear clothes and there is no danger of beasts, then it is nothing more than an ostentation to keep the smoke-fire lit.

Those who conduct serious scientific research need solitude to avoid disturbance. In earlier times the serious researchers of spirituality also needed work centers and laboratories to carry out their research. For this the solitude of caves in regions like Himalaya would suit them just right. When they would want to disseminate results of their findings they would embark on long pilgrimages to sacred places. This life style was adopted based upon sound reasoning. However, several instances of worthless and blind imitations of this life style can be found today. To make a show of their arduous penance people name the basement of buildings in cities as a 'dark cave' and live there wasting away their time.

The tradition of applying ash on the body was popular earlier because the layer of ash would protect the body from heat and cold. This would reduce the need for excessive clothing. Now, for those who can have enough clothes and other means of protection from temperature-variation, what is the need to apply ash for ostentation? When barbers could not be found in the forests earlier, the hair of men would grow long and had to be tied up. Now what is the need to imitate this by fixing fake hair on the head with pins? All this only creates delusions in the mind of naïve public.

For those who resided in forests it was convenient to use shells of fruits like coconut to hold water. But now, when pots of brass/steel are easily available these should be used both for convenience and cleanliness. Other equipments like tongs, three pronged weapons (*trishul*), axe etc might have had utility in ancient times as tools of protection from wild animals in the forests. Why should these be regarded as symbols of ascetic lives or attire of *swamis*? The fake *swamis* keep such tools only to befool and trick others.

The principle behind pilgrimages was traveling on foot to meet more and more people on the way and spread the thoughts of righteous living and spirituality among them. But when this purpose is completely lost now, it is wrong to waste time by visiting ponds and lakes on the pretext of washing away sins and that too without paying for the train/bus ticket!

There is no place for pretension and weird dressing in spirituality. When the ideals and actions of yester era are forgotten then what use it is to adopt external ostentations? We must not let the profound knowledge of spirituality become a matter of general ridicule by adopting awkward behavior or escaping away from duties. Instead we must work on reviving its great traditions while living lives in normal ways.

In the name of spirituality many fake gurus and swamis are seen today living luxurious lives on the funds donated/collected by their blind flowers. They should know that the right to live on community resources is reserved only for those who devote every moment of their lives for the selfless service, welfare and enlightenment of the society.

Simplicity, sensitivity and sagacity are essential characteristics of spiritual ascent. The seekers and masters of spirituality must cultivate these in their thoughts and deeds.

A Life Imbibed with Spirituality | 5

When the basic principles that guide an experiment are right, then the results of the experiment have to be satisfying. Erudite writers of venerated scriptures have not written unfounded exaggerations. The enlightened men of yore chose to present the essence of their experiences in the form of scriptures; there is no possibility of baseless hyperbole in their statements. What is required is that the basic, tenets must be properly understood, and then experiments must be conducted firmly based upon those. If this process is not followed and the results are not as good as expected, then surely the fault has to lie in our own methods and interpretations.

Need For An Example:

In present times, simply stating principles cannot convince. None would be satisfied and would follow the path of spirituality unless the claimed results are authentically demonstrated in reality. So there is an important need to present an example here, an example of a person who treaded this path and rose to great heights. We choose a person about whom every stated fact can be verified. (There are several so-called great men of the past about whom their followers associate many great stories and amazing incidents. But of these narrations how many are really true cannot be verified.) We present the example of an extraordinary personality, during whose life several exceptional incidents unfolded which were witnessed by others as well. Each such incident can be independently verified by any one to get convinced of its authenticity. His whole life span was a living proof that spirituality is a pure science and that its accomplishments are in no way inferior to the achievements of material sciences.

This great personality was Pandit Shriram Sharma Acharya, the founder patron of Pragya Abhiyan and Yug Nirman Mission. Glimpses of some divine potentials, endeavors and achievements of this seer sage of our times have been cited in some of the following chapters of this book. Here we outline the biography of his spiritual journey.

The eighty years of his life are akin to a book of eighty pages, each page of which is a shining illustration of the application of science of spirituality and its outcomes. The regal path he treaded upon can be an inspiration for millions of others. Anyone can achieve great heights in this world and beyond by following him, and can reach glorious goals of human life. Here we shall mention only those few facets of his life that illustrate relevant facts, principles and experiments.

Incarnation of Spirituality:

The important part of the story of Acharyaji's life begins when he was 15 years old. While he was praying in the early hours of auspicious Vasant Panchami day (the 5th lunar day of spring season by Hindu calendar), a divine human being (his guru in this life) appeared before him in a sublime form. His divine being appeared within a bright aura of light. The young boy was totally scared to see the spectacle, but the divine human form assured him and said, "I have appeared before you now to guide you in this life. I have been with you in several previous births. In your long journey of multiple lives you have proven your worthiness and so you did not have to go in search of light. Instead, the light itself has come to you to provide guidance."

The young boy was still skeptical. He began to wonder whether what he was seeing was a ghost or just an illusion of his mind! The divine being understood the boy's confused state of mind and did something so that the boy's realizations would arise from within. He was asked to close his eyes and watch his previous births. Entire lifetimes of previous births in the past 700 years were shown to him. In each of these births he had followed the path of spirituality and each birth was one step forward to prove his worthiness. There were about ten lifetimes in this period, of which three were of special significance: those of Kabir, Samarth Guru Ramdas and Ramkrishna Paramhans. All these lives followed the same path guided by the same light, even though the methods adopted kept changing depending upon the requirements of the prevailing times. Though this vision was just like a day dream, its effect was as if it was all real and true. The boy attained realization and was convinced.

A question now arose in his mind, what was the purpose of this birth of his? Before he could ask, his guru himself began to elaborate. The entire plan of this lifetime was laid out before him, right up to his death. To attain the strength and capability necessary for the plan he was instructed to follow specific guidelines for 24 years. In this period he was told to live on rolled bread (*roti*) made from barley and buttermilk only, for self- purification and strengthening of will. He was also told to play an active role in Indian freedom movement while continuing his *sādhanā*.

This was the unexpressed aspect of his penance. For the expressed aspect, he was told to weave his life with the tenets of *Upāsanā, Sādhanā* and *Arādhanā*. All the needs for his livelihood were already available to him from ancestral property. Whatever charity and good deeds he did in previous births returned back to him in the form of heirloom in this birth. This provided him a good opportunity to devote the entire life to *Upāsanā, Sādhanā* and *Arādhanā*.

Upāsanā literally means "sitting near"; as sitting near the fire makes one feel warm, similarly *upāsanā* of God, if practised sincerely through pure heart, generates a subtle proximity with divinity. The devotional practices of *upāsanā* are meant to experience the proximity and light of divinity and prepare the inner being for a complete surrender to God. Acharya Shriram Sharma practiced *upāsanā* of Gayatri – the primordial force of Supreme Creation, the Goddess of divine intellect and spiritual evolution, with complete mental engrossment and devotion. He merged himself and became one with his deity, like a rivulet with a river, like firewood with fire, like a drop of water in the vast ocean. With his perseverant dedication he achieved oneness with God.

The second effort was *sādhanā* – the process of refining oneself through self-restraint. His efforts for self-cleansing were akin to washing of clothes by a washer man, or trimming of gardens by a gardener, or training of wild animals by a circus trainer. He adopted the principle of strictness towards self and kindness towards others. He waged a war to subdue the passion for materialistic possession, the attachment towards dear ones, and the obsession towards establishing self-importance. He combined this process of purification and improvement with sustained efforts to gain wisdom. He continued this *sādhanā* of acquiring virtues and discarding base tendencies all through his life.

The third aspect of living a spiritual life was *arādhanā* – the selfless service of the society and kindness and benevolence towards others. He whole-heartedly devoted his energy, his time, his influence, his talents and personal resources for upliftment of others. The tenet of *arādhanā* has two aspects. The first one is to uplift the downtrodden, to assuage others' pain, and to never let an opportunity to help and comfort others go by. The second aspect is to cultivate virtuousness and root out evil tendencies from the society. For these, creative endeavors as well as a constant battle against evil needs to go on hand in hand. Like his *sādhanā*, Acharyaji strived all his life to enhance his *arādhanā* for creating an enlightened society, a new world.

Spiritual lives have always been cast in this mould of *upāsanā*, *sādhanā* and *arādhanā*. The dual aspects of penance (*tapa*) for self-cleansing, and yoga with righteousness have been their characteristic. Acharyaji's whole life was also directed towards this path. He adopted the process of self-study (*swādhyāya*), company of noble beings (*satsang*), pondering over illumined thoughts (*chintan*) and contemplation and reflection (*manan*) all his life. This process expanded his wisdom to start activities relevant to the present needs, to garner support for his mission and to guide his endeavors to their goal.

Because of the attention he paid to details and the extreme care he took while planning, he never failed to attain what he set out for. It wasn't that he never faced obstacles. Whenever righteousness begins to grow, evil raises its head and tries to subdue and hurt those who side with it. But when goodness stands firm on its grounds, badness has to recoil back. Acharya ji also had to face innumerable trials and tribulations, but he overcame them all. These refined his personality that shone like gold refined in fire.

Call from the Himalayas:

When Acharya ji proved his worthiness through his long and sincere penance, and proved his resolve, bravery, restraint and discipline in difficult times, divine blessings showered upon him from subtle worlds and gratified him. His divine guru who came to him in his adolescence, took notice of his achievements after 25 years and decided to bestow upon him a large portion of his own powers as boons. He called upon Acharya ji to visit his abode in far and remote regions of Himalayas.

Acharya ji visited Himalayas three times. He was asked to travel to Kailash-Mansarovar region in Sumeru mountain ranges within the boundaries of Nandanavan Valley–Uttarakhand. He was introduced to great *rishis* of Himalayas, who in astral bodies even now are carrying out their penance in the divine caves of this region. He was provided with provisions and a place for shelter in this remote area.

In these visits Acharya ji was explained what steps he would need to take to fulfill the needs of creating a new era. He was told when and in what form would divine cooperation help him to attain success, what kind of efforts he would need to put in personally, and how would the task of searching out higher living souls be done. He was also assured that in every difficult situation divine assistance would be there to help him.

The Grand Plan of Creation of New Era:

The divine *rishis* bestowed upon Acharya ji with the following future activities –

1. Establishment of two prime centers for changing the era on the banks of holy rivers Ganga and Yamuna.

2. Launching a search for refined and purified souls, and awaken and prepare them for creative endeavours.

3. Creation of a great organization that would spread the message of era-changing in people's conscience.

4. Creation of religious establishments throughout the world that would act as centres for reviving the era of truth

5. Organizing a big conference of all the divine souls located, to introduce them with each other and define a way ahead for them.

6. Making scriptures and literature written by *rishis* easily available to all.

7. Extensive creation of literature for the new era and their translation and spread in other languages

8. Designing and running a training course curriculum for creators of the new era

9. Clarifying basic tenets of spirituality and integrating science and spirituality in a constructive way, thus convincing modern day intellectuals and scientists about the relevance of spirituality.

10. Reviving the science of Gayatri mantra and *Yagya* from oblivion and to reestablish the dignity they deserve.

11. Reinstate the tradition of *Vānprastha* Ashram.

12. Establishing the dignity of Ayurveda the ancient system of Indian medicine by the great *rishis* Charak and Sushrut.

13. Spreading the consciousness of new era to all parts of the globe.

14. Make preparations for *Pragyā Puraścharaṇ* to refine the sublime atmosphere and environment.

These were the fourteen activities that Acharya ji was asked to actively pursue. He was also asked to gather support and resources for these with sincere efforts. Though, due to the influence of prevailing times, human mind today is enslaved by base and lowly tendencies, the seeds of greatness and high ideals are never completely destroyed. Even today great souls live upon the earth. The only task was to search for them with determination. This effort was akin to the efforts of divers who search and bring out glittering pearls from the deep seas. Such a daunting task had to be accomplished by the combined efforts of Acharya ji and his guru.

The whole plan of Acharya ji's multifaceted illustrious life may be divided into three stages. The first stage was to develop a strong and resolute personality – chiseled and illumined by spiritual glow, by practising *upāsanā, sādhanā* (including the super- *sādhanā* of twenty-four Gayatri *Mahapurashścharaṇs*) and *arādhanā*.

The second stage was implementation of mission-based reformative and constructive programmes according to the fourteen-point plan.

The third stage comprised of activities that are being carried out in the realms beyond human perception. In these the adversities of the invisible world are being turned to favorable. He is working to save the earth from wide spread disasters and save humanity from total destruction. The *Yug Sandhi Purashścharaṇ sādhanā* – of awakening collective consciousness – initiated, inspired and guided by him would help in creating an ambience of enhanced spiritual energy suitable for changing the era for a brighter future for all. In his subtle and astral forms, he is also influencing and motivating awakened beings all over the world to participate in the innumerable activities for the creation of a new era.

Acharya ji shed the sheath of his physical body on 2nd June 1990 and has now become active in his subtle and causal bodies. In his direct supervision the first two stages of his life-plan were successfully accomplished. The experiments he conducted upon himself and upon the society bore two results. The faith of common masses on the principles of spirituality was reestablished, and the seeds of righteousness and virtuousness that he planted in the society began to grow and spread. In the last five years of his life he had reached the pinnacle of the *sādhanā* of *sukśmīkaraṇa*. Some of the aspects of this *sādhanā* of his have been touched upon in Chapters 8 and 9. His immense power is now on the verge of creating huge perturbations that would destroy the current dilapidated structure and would build a new society and a new world.

The foundational principles of spiritual progress that were integral part of his eminent life should be followed by every aspirant of enlightened ascent. Some of these are highlighted in the next Chapter.

Additional Reading:

1. Chetana Ki Shikhara Yatra Vols. I to IV (by Pranav Pandya and Jyotrimaya), Sri Vedmata Gayatri Trust, Shantikunj, Haridwar, 2003+

2. My Life – Its Legacy and Message (English Translation of the Autobiography of Pandit Shriram Sharma Acharya), Sri Vedmata Gayatri Trust, Shantikunj, Haridwar, 3rd Ed. 2004.

Absolute Principle of "Sow and Reap" | 6

The fundamental tenet of "first sow and then reap" is universally recognized in every walk of life. Every facet of Nature, every discipline of science affirms it. It is given prime importance in the science of spirituality.

We all know that a farmer ploughs the fields, sows the seeds, works hard to irrigate and guard the saplings. It is only after the hard labor of days and nights and patience that he gets to harvest the valuable crops at the right time. Students work hard on their studies for the whole academic year. Only then they earn good grades in the exams and get admitted to higher studies of their choice; their meticulous efforts pave the way for their steady rise and for admirable successes in their professions or scholarly achievements. Chance also favors only the prepared mind. Not only the inventions but the great discoveries of modern science too were made only by those who engrossed their minds deep in related thoughts and experiments. A businessman takes risk, puts in his initial capital, skills, planning and assiduity to launch new entrepreneurial projects, trades, industries, etc. His prosperity increases with success and profit earned by his industrious efforts. Similar is the case for ascent and accomplishments on every front of life. The principle of "*Siddhi* from *Sādhanā*" evinces this universal truth in the fields of spirituality.

Great spiritual masters, *siddhas* or *yogis* acquire the supernatural powers only after arduous endeavors of self-control, ascetic disciplines, penance, self-refinement and thorough practice of the specific *yoga* and spiritual pursuits. Success in the field of spirituality is not attained simply by cramming some religious text, talking high in impressive voice or posing as a great sage or saint. One cannot fool people for too long by fake practices. A seeker of spirituality has to walk the talk. The outer as well as inner spheres of his life, his external as well as internal personality, have to become pure, serene and illumined by the glow of virtuous sentiments, thoughts and conduct.

The path to spiritual attainments is quite slippery, as it often deals with inner experiences and subtle facts. People are often tempted by the supernormal potentials cited in the scriptures and in immature attempts to achieve spiritual success, they hesitate in stepping on this path and take up shortcuts like superficial prayers and ritualistic practices. Some simply run away from home and normal life, without realizing that it is the bond of selfish attachment, ego and avarice that needs to be broken without escaping from the duties of the present life. They end up with failures and frustration. After all, how can significant success be attained without putting in careful efforts in the right directions? These failed men either spend their lives crying over their failures or some of the smarter ones 'adopt' the attire of *sannyāsis*, form their cults and befool naïve men by performing cheap magic tricks in the name of *siddhis*. They might succeed in attracting a few innocents by exploiting their intellectual immaturity, blind faith and emotional fragility or by gathering greedy 'disciples' who want to 'book' a seat in '*swarg*' (heavens) by simple means or who are desperate to get rid of hard-times and want to gain riches and powers in no time. Their fallacies and misdeeds often create misconception in the minds of the rational thinkers especially if the latter do not know what spirituality really is – and thus distort and devalue this preeminent science of consciousness-force and conscience.

The noble Gurus and the true seekers of the light of spirituality are extra cautious and observe great patience in the time-testing pursuit of *sādhanā. Siddhis* are never their goals; these are bestowed upon them naturally by the eternal law of Nature – "as you sow, so will you reap". The life of seer-sage Pandit Shriram Sharma Acharya, who is among the noblest spiritual gurus of the caliber of the *Vedic Rishis,* is a remarkable exemplar of this fact.

Pandit Shriram Sharma aimed to decipher the deeper depths of the science of spirituality to verify its applicability for the ascent of mankind and auspicious benefit of the world. He therefore scrupulously studied and experimented with Raja Yoga, Hatha Yoga, Mantra Yoga, Laya Yoga, Kundalini Yoga, Gyana Yoga, Karma Yoga, Bhakti Yoga and other disciplines of yoga *sādhanās* that have emanated from the ancient Indian Philosophy. He also followed *sādhanās* originated or spread outside India. He discovered that the essence of each of these is that each path to spirituality begins with self-refinement and self-discipline. Without these one can never achieve spiritual elevation. His own life was a living evidence of divine transmutation of human self by devout spiritual endeavors.

Those who do not pass the acid test of purification of character and chiseled refinement of sentiments, thoughts and conduct, but aspire for supernatural faculties like *śaktipāta, kuṇḍalinī jāgaraṇa*, vision of God, etc make a mockery of the whole discipline of spirituality and end up in failure. Their attempts are no better than fantasy of a day-dreamer or of an innocent child who wants to jump and get a post-graduate degree without passing the primary school. Howsoever loud he may cry or throw tantrums, the education system cannot be altered to fulfill such unreasonable demands.

As per the sublime guidance of the Himalayan Rishis (Vedic Sages), Pt. Shriram Sharma Acharya dedicated all his *sādhanās* – including the supreme *sādhanās* of Savitri and Gayatri – for altruistic welfare of all beings. This was like sowing the supreme quality seeds in the most fertile field that enriched his mission with divine beatitudes.

Sowing of good quality seeds in a fertile land returns thousand fold. Look at the blossoming crops of wheat, barley, maze, etc! Each seed (grain) that loses its own existence to give birth to new saplings eventually generates several thousands of new grains. Look at the mighty trees of mango, blackberry etc produced from a tiny seed! What a formidable return of Nature! The trees offer hundreds of new fruits (containing new seeds too) every year for so many years and the cycle continues.... The small offering of fist full of rice gifted by poor Sudama to his childhood friend Lord Krishna or the few wild plums whole-heartedly offered by tribal woman Shabari to Lord Ram returned back to them enormously, and continue to remind us age-after-age, that selfless goodwill and good deeds lead to immortal glory.

Pt Shriram Sharma sincerely adopted this principle of "Sow and Reap" in his life. He endeavored the highest levels of arduous spiritual experiments on himself but did not keep the great benefits for himself. Neither did he demonstrate or boast of his supernormal powers to gain popularity and honors. He preferred devoting his talents and potentials for the awakening of masses, for people's social, mental and spiritual upliftment. He regarded altruistic service as the noblest kind of worship. We may not find another example of this sort in human-history, that a seer-sage of *rishi*-caliber has dedicated every moment of his life for the welfare of the masses and has also provided adept guidance and strength to one and all for their moral, mental, intellectual and spiritual growth. Not only that, he also pioneered a unique approach to integration of science and spirituality.

The physical body, strength, intelligence, thought-power and talents are all bequests of God. Only the worldly possessions, if any, gained by somebody using these gifts of God, may be attributed to as his own. However, the worldly success or resources too cannot be accredited to one person alone because many others in his family, work place, or in the society at large, play a direct or indirect role in his achievements. Thus, in several respects, one owes to the Almighty and to the world for his talents, powers and resources. Part of these should be therefore used for the betterment of others as well. Sympathetic support to the worried, the helpless and downtrodden; courage and hope to the depressed, the broken ones; and thoughtful directions to elevate those seeking the righteous path, etc should necessarily be offered by those who are better off.

Sowing the Seeds of Material Wealth:

Sevā-sādhanā (self-less service of all beings) was an integral part of Pt. Shriram Sharma Acharya's life. Whatever those who were blessed by his help and support have expressed, indicates the enormity of his kind grace, which saw no bounds. His inner urge for the wellbeing of all and his unflinching dedication to this benevolent cause glorified his spiritual efforts more. He adopted an austere life-style of a true Brahmin and devoted himself to social service as religiously as to advanced *sādhanās*. His writings and discourses also contributed in this regard and continue to enlighten and guide the lives of millions.

Right from his childhood he was seen busy trying his level best to support the helpless, diseased and old people in the colony irrespective of their caste-creed or social lineage. His spiritual *sādhanā* began in full stream in 1926, at the age of 15 years. For the next 24 years he successfully accomplished the 24 *Mahāpuraścaranas* of Gayatri. During this period, he followed ascetic disciplines (*c.f.* chapter 5). He also actively participated in the non-violent freedom struggle of India and in the grass-root social reformation movement of eradication of casteism, gender-bias, superstitions, blind customs, religious fundamentalism, etc.

He donated all his share of ancestral property in opening a girls' higher secondary school at village Anwalkheda (his birth place in Agra District) and established Gayatri Tapobhumi Ashram at Mathura. Keeping bare minimum for his children's education (in state-run schools) and for two meals and two pairs of handloom clothes for himself and family, every paise of whatever money he had was donated to the mission of transforming mankind for the brighter future (*Yug Nirman Yojna*). Since their marriage in 1946, his wife Smt. Bhagavati Devi Sharma (Revered Mataji) also marched with him giving her full cooperation at every step. Revered Mataji also sold her jewelry for the growth of this mission and its expansion in the form of the global centre at Shantikunj, Haridwar. This renouncement of personal wealth, selfish attachments, self-comforts, and unconditional sacrifice for the society further empowered the saintly spirits of this *rishi*-couple and led to amazing expansion of their divine mission in the form of All World Gayatri Pariwar — a grand family of millions of their disciples and followers. What could be a better example of "sow whatever you have and harvest all you want"?

Sowing the Seeds of Intellect:

Another exemplar of Pandit Shriram Sharma Acharya's supramental talents and sainthood stands on the intellectual front. He was born in a highly reputed, well off family. His father was a renowned scholar of Sanskrit. The divine Indian Culture and its preaching and precious virtuous values were inculcated in him by his parents from his early childhood. Eminent personalities like Pandit Madan Mohan Malviya and Dr. S. Radhakrishanan – the first President of India were among his father's friends. His family inherited hundreds of acres of agricultural and residential lands in Anwalalkheda. Shriram was exceptionally bright since the childhood. Soon after Pt. Malviya ji performed his thread ceremony and initiated the knowledge of Gayatri Mantra to this child of 9 years, Shriram visited the library of the Banaras Hindu University (BHU). By then he was taught only the Hindi and Sanskrit languages. He not only read but also thoroughly grasped the knowledge inscribed in all the volumes and books (written in these languages) available in the BHU library at that time. His supernormal memory retained everything throughout his life. (During his participation in India's freedom movement he also learnt English and Urdu. With the unfolding of his extraordinary intelligence, later on his associates discovered that he was able to grasp the thoughts expressed mentally, orally or in writing in every language of the world).

The visible contribution of the donation of his time and super-intelligence to the world in the eighty years of his physical life is itself more than what the most eminent brains and skilled hands would contribute in perhaps eight-hundred years. He translated the entire Vedic texts (including the 4 Vedas, 108 Upanishads and 18 Puranas) in lucid Hindi for the benefit of the masses and wrote over 2400 books on almost all aspects pertaining to human life. He also managed publication of two enlightening monthly magazines "Akhand Jyoti" and "Yug Nirman Yojna". There are no parallels to sagacious and eloquent writings of this kind on topics encompassing a wide range – from day to day matters of personal, familial and social development to deepest depth of spirituality and science. On an average, his routine had only about 6 hours for himself: 2

hours of sound sleep, 4 hours of early morning for Gayatri S³dhan³. He wrote for about 8 hours per day. Rest of the time was for activities of mass awakening and social uplifting.

Sowing the Seeds of Spiritual Acumen in Science & Culture:

It is not easy for everyone to control the agility of mind and meditate upon the inner light, divine thoughts or go into trance. The devotional methods (*Upāsanā*) of prayers, rituals of worship, *japa* and *dhyāna* and the Vedic sacraments (in the original form) of *śodas samskāras*[11] were devised by spiritual masters of yore keeping in mind the nature of human mind. These practices help emotional linkage with divinity represented in the object of devotion and thereby provide psychological conditioning and also enable the awakening and positive channelization of faith. Yug Rishi Pandit Shriram Sharma revived these facets of the spiritual culture.

In the light of the great sages and glorious spiritual masters of all ages and his own experiences with the super science of Gayatri and Yagya, he initiated millions of people from all walks of the society to performing Yagya and practising Gayatri Sadhana with the support of *japa* of the Gayatri *Mantra*, which is a scientific mode of mental engrossment and emotional soothing for refinement of thought-process and inculcation of sensitivity [2-4]. He also taught and showed the importance of *upāsanā*[5] in invocation of divinity within and established *Yagya* as a feasible mode of healthcare and environmental purification both at physical and mental levels[6-11].

Sowing the Seeds of Love:

His Bhakti Yoga was unified with experiencing God in human sentiments, in love and compassion. Some people may consider *'bhakti'* (devotion) as certain rituals of worship and devotional singing and crying before the deity and loving the deity. But that is not true *bhakti* unless the devotee's heart is full of pure love for every being. Pt. Shriram Sharmaji's heart pulsated with love and sensitivity for every one. He thus was devoted to true *"navadhā bhakti"* every moment. The spiritual glow of his personality awakened others' intrinsic faith in divinity. He and Rev. Mataji distributed infinite love upon every one. Indeed, they proved that the highest goal of *bhakti* is beatifying love, which includes limitless mercy and unconditional giving and giving....

They used to meet thousands of people every day and affectionately listen to all the problems and queries of each visitor. They offered fulfilling solutions, mental strength, guidance, and support to every one. The number of those guided and blessed by them via postal correspondence every day was no less. Any one who has ever met or written to them has not felt dissatisfaction, adversity or helplessness thereafter; their beatifying encouragement has inspired and enabled everyone to move ahead on the righteous path of progress. Even several volumes (like the Vedic Scriptures of "Puranas") would be less if only a summary was written of the experiences of those blessed by Gurudev Pandit. Shriram Sharma ji and Mata ji.

The Harvest:

Benevolent donation of everything they had, their material wealth, intellectual faculty, love and time for the society returned manifold. They received generous cooperation of millions of men and women from all walks of the society which advanced and expanded their 100-points project of social, intellectual, ethical and spiritual transformation of mankind and awakening of divinity hidden in the human heart. Establishment of majors institutions with thousands of branches (*c.f.* Chapter 7) of Gayatri Pariwar in different parts of India and abroad, whole-hearted participation of millions in the grand *yagyas*, nullification of the crisis of faith in the younger-generation, loosening of the tight grip of casteism, nearly a million ideal marriages without dowry in the regions notorious for social evils and rigid customs in India, and revival of the *Rishi* Culture, etc and global recognition of the divine culture (*c.f.* Chapters 7 and 8) are visible evidences of the manifold returns of their goodwill and noble initiatives.

Small donations by millions have led to the development of gigantic corpus for the mission's grand projects — including establishment of a unique university on the lines of the prestigious ancient universities of Nalanda and Takshashila with due incorporation, in scientific approach, of the needs of the present era.

Immersion of all emotions and personal aspirations in the cosmic self led to showering of divine boons upon this angelic couple. Manifestation of these boons was visibly expressed in three forms — first, absolute contentment and unalloyed, unperturbed joy in their hearts, second, reverence, whole-hearted cooperation and dedication of millions of people across the globe and third, divine support at every step that miraculously eliminated all adversities, attacks and obstacles in the path of their mission. God lived with them like their body-guard and guide and His limitless grace showered upon them from all directions.

References/Additional Reading:

1. *ṣodaśa Samskāra Vivechana.* Pandit Shriram Sharma Acharya Samagra Vangmaya Vol. 33, Akhand Jyoti Sansthan, Mathura (India), 1995.

2. *Śabda Brahṁ Nāda Brahṁ.* Pandit Shriram Sharma Acharya Samagra Vangmaya Vol. 18, Akhand Jyoti Sansthan, Mathura (India), 1995.

3. Eternity of Sound and the Science of Mantras. (Translation of some Hindi texts of ref. no. [2] above). Yuganter Chetana Press, Haridwar, 2003.

4. *Gāyatrī Sādhanā Kī Vaigyānika Praṣṭhabhūmi.* Pandit Shriram Sharma Acharya Samagra Vangmaya Vol. 14, Akhand Jyoti Sansthan, Mathura (India), 1995.

5. The Meaning Purpose and Benefits of Worship. (Translation of the Hindi book *"Upāsanā Kā Tatva Darśana Aur Swarūpa"*, by Pt. Shriram Sharma Acharya), Shri Vedmata Gayatri Trust Shantikunj, Haridwar, 2005. ISBN: 81-8255-013-0

6. *Yagya Kā Gyāna-Vigyāna.* Pandit Shriram Sharma Acharya Samagra Vangmaya Vol. 25, Akhand Jyoti Sansthan, Mathura (India), 1995.

7. *Yagya Eka Samagra Upachāra Prakriyā.* Pandit Shriram Sharma Acharya Samagra Vangmaya Vol. 26, Akhand Jyoti Sansthan, Mathura (India), 1995.

8. Some Investigations into the Chemical and pharmaceutical Aspects of *Yagyopathy.* PhD Thesis, by Meenakshi Raghuvanshi, Dev Sanskriti Univ., Haridwar 2006.

). *Yagyopathy* Vs Oral and I.V. Drug Administration: Evaluation for Pulmonary Tuberculosis using Compartment Modeling. (Research Paper by Joshi R. R., Raghuvanshi M. and Pandya P.). *J. Biological Systems*, 2006, Vol. 14(3), pp. 463-489.

10. Yagyopathic Herbal Treatment of Pulmonary Tuberculosis Symptoms – A Clinical Trial. (Research Paper by Raghuvanshi M., Pandya P. and Joshi R. R.). *Alter. & Compl. Therapies*, 2004, Vol. 10 (2), pp. 101-105.

11. A Quality modeling and Non-Conventional Solutions to the Environmental Pollution Problems with Reference to the Vedic Sciences. PhD Thesis, by Mamta Saxena, Dev Sanskriti Univ., Haridwar, 2006.

Milestones of a Divine Mission | 7

Pandit Shriram Sharma Acharya's life was exceptonal in all terms. During his lifetime several extraordinary events unfolded which can convince any skeptic of the force of spirituality. Here are a few of Acharya ji's amazing achievements.

The Grand *Yagya* of 1958:

Acharya ji had completed twenty-four *Mahāpuraścharaṇas* (*sādhanā* of 2.4 million Gayri mantra *japa*) in twenty-four years. This had to be followed up with a grand *yagya* in which 240000 *ahuti*s (sacrificial herbal offerings to fire in *yagya*) were to be offered. It was decided that at least one hundred thousand Gayatri *sādhaks* from all over the country should be invited for a grand *yagya* programme. A big *yagyashala* (hall) consisting of one thousand *yagyakund* (pits for sacrificial fire) should be prepared and the requisite number of *ahuti*s could then be offered by these *sadhus* in five days. This yagya was planned for the *kartik* month of year 1958 from 11th to 15th day of bright half of the lunar month.

The big questions were how to gather so many participants for the *yagya*, how to arrange for firewood, ghee, herbal materials for offerings, tents for *yagyashala* and discourses, and how to arrange for accommodation, food, water, sanitation, electricity etc. for all the invitees. There was a need for large grounds for erecting tents. Immense monetary resources were needed for even simple tasks like cooking and serving food. And then there were other considerations like how to send invitations to so many people, and how to arrange for transport for hundreds-of-thousands of people to arrive together on a day and then return together on another.

Acharya ji had only rupees five thousand with him then and the estimated expenses for the *yagya* were of the order of rupees five million. Ordinary minds cannot even imagine how this could ever be done. Especially at that time when Acharya ji had never raised any public funds earlier and had a support of less than a dozen volunteers. Several days were spent in thinking and planning but nothing concrete could be worked out.

Time came and each problem got solved with divine intervention on its own, one by one. Invitation letters reached to Gayatri *sādhaks* in every corner of the country. They arrived at the right time – one hundred thousand invitees, along with at least three hundred thousand more onlookers. Arrangements were made to provide food and accommodation to four hundred thousand people. The whole task was accomplished with such beauty and skillfulness that in seven miles radius, seven towns named after the famed seven-*rishis* of India were set up. The long rows of tents were more impressive then those that are set up during the large Kumbha fairs. Food was prepared in seven large public kitchens and served free of charge to all the visitors day and night. None of those who came was left without food and shelter. Everyone orderly paid sacrificial offerings in the *yagyashala*. Not a single incident of stealing took place. The food supply from storehouses became inexhaustible. Having heard the news of such a grand function, people from nearby towns rushed in to see the spectacle. The entire population of onlookers exceeded one million. Everyone had only one thing to say that such a grand and well-organized *yagya* experiment had never taken place earlier. Thousands of loud speakers and electricity generators were utilized to maintain order; each satellite town had telephone connections. Thousands of volunteers came forward and contributed their might. Donation boxes were kept everywhere, small change collected in them became enough to bear several expenses. There was no dearth of any kind of resources.

The whole event can be called the first grand miracle of spirituality. It was as if some divine power compelled all the visitors, volunteers, managers and assistants to witness and play a role in this splendid event.

Genesis of Gayatri Pariwar:

Gayatri Pariwar is a very large worldwide family of people who accept Acharya ji as their guru and follow the path he walked. This pariwar was also created during the 1958 yagya. All the invitees for grand *yagya* gathered in the discourse hall and became the first members of 'Gayatri Pariwar'. The membership fee was kept as one rosary of Gayatri *japa* and the donation of one hour of time per day for organizational activities and spreading awareness to masses. The huge mission came into being overnight. During the yagya, programmes were formulated for furthering the ideology of *upāsanā, sādhanā* and *arādhanā* in local contexts. It was not just the whole *yagya* that was magical, what was much more amazing was the creation of such a big organization with one hundred thousand members, overnight. At the time of farewell, all the members of this newly formed family vowed to devote their time and best efforts for the planned activities. This family has now grown to include several million people from across the world, from all walks of human society.

Another great miracle in the life of Acharya ji was the cooperation and support he got from so many emotionally attached, hard working individuals. They worked with him as close associates and never asked for any form of pay. This great association began with Bhagawati Devi Sharma, revered wife of Acharya ji. Everyone called her Mata ji (beloved mother). The day she came into Acharya ji's life she became like his shadow. She took the entire onus of managing the mission upon her shoulders. She distributed the nectar of motherly love and affection upon all those who came in her contact. The combination of highly evolved intellect (*pragyā*) of Acharya ji and unflinching pure faith (*śraddhā*) of Mata ji created a great magic. Together they won the hearts of millions. Whoever came in their close contact got convinced that he or she has to play a role in the momentous task of reconstruction of the era. Mata ji's disposition to service, her love, simplicity and managerial acumen had such an impact that all members of the organization began to consider themselves as her sons and daughters. These feelings and love have grown stronger with the years. Acharya ji used to say that Mata ji is like the holy river Ganga; she is divinity herself that has incarnated in feminine form. More than half the credit for Acharya ji's accomplishments must go to Mata ji. This divine association of two great souls can be termed no less than a magic of spirituality.

When the brightness began to spread all around, innumerable people with evolved sentiments became a part of the mission. All the dedicated workers who are currently working at various major organizations of the mission are at least graduate and previously well employed. There are several thousands of people in the mission who are working in diverse regions of the country. All these devoted men and women have a single-minded devotion towards their mission. At least half of these workers are those who bear their own expenses and sustain with their conserved monetary funds. The mission provides for basic needs (including children's education) of the remaining who were not that well-off. No one working for the mission thinks of accumulating money for future or emergency. If an emergency comes, mission provides funds to fulfill those needs. This can be called as the modern and purposeful edition of the tradition of sages and Brahmins. These days it is almost impossible to find such a large number of devoted, idealistic individuals in any organization. The gathering of such talented and devoted individuals under one umbrella simply reminds of the Congress party during Indian freedom movement or of the monk groups constituted by Lord Buddha.

Gayatri Pariwar created by Acharya ji has grown manifold. There are six major institutions associated with Gayatri Pariwar. A brief look at the activities in these institutes would help in understanding Gayatri Pariwar's extensive efforts to bring about descent of heaven upon earth. All these institutes have come up on expansive pieces of land. Their construction was started with Acharya ji's personal funds that he generated by selling off all his ancestral property. This fund was no more than one hundred thousand rupees, which is a very small sum, especially when one looks at the impressive buildings constructed at these places. Acharya ji had a principle of never asking for funds or seeking money from the rich, or the government. All the members of this vast family contributed a handful of grains and ten paise daily for the mission. Several individuals contributed for the cause of their own free will. This is how all the institutions have been built. Each institute is playing a major role in the construction of a new era.

Gayatri Teerth (Pilgrimage Center) - Shantikunj:

Shantikunj is located about 6 km from Haridwar railway station on the road towards Rishikesh in Uttarakhand state. Shantikunj has emerged over the years as a unique center and fountain-head of the global movement of Yug Nirman Yojana (Movement for the Reconstruction of the Era) for moral-spiritual regeneration in the light of hoary Indian heritage. Visitors of all faiths & linkages visit this sacred center for their spiritual upliftment all the year round.

The most important role played by Shantikunj is in conducting several training programs for reinstatement of moral, cultural and ethical values, integration of various faiths and sects into one common thought process, and channelization of energies of youths. Amongst these, the regular ones are: (i) nine-day training of Sanjeewani Vidyaa which is a comprehensive course on the art of living and art of relating, (ii) one month training of Yug Shilpi and Parivraajak which are training camps for refinement of personality and learning the art of serving the society and leading reformation activities. The latter programme has generated hundreds of thousands of men and women who work in the society for its development. Occasional trainings of officers and employees of Government, local bodies, corporations, banks etc. are also organized for teaching how to lead elegant life style, organizational management, efficient working methodology, managing personal health etc. Free training programmes are also conducted related to agriculture, horticulture, dairy and herbal production for selected village folk for self-employment generation. All these trainings aim at the all round development of the nation and integration of the country by inducing noble sentiments in the minds of individuals by adoption of scientific ways of spirituality.

Shantikunj acts as a centre for guiding various Gayatri Pariwar activities like social reformation activities, psycho-social engineering, disaster management, self-reliant development of rural India, revival of Vedic culture, innovative research in ayurveda, ascent, empowerment of women and so on. Shantikunj has a vast network of about 4000 Shaktipeeths-Pragya Peeths (Centers of knowledge and Divine power), 25000 Pragya Sansthans & 30,000 Swadhyaya Mandals (self-study groups) etc., which regularly organize spiritual discussions, discourses, discussions on various problems in their areas to advance the noble cause of the Mission.

Near the entrance of Shantikunj are Prakhar Pragya and Sajal Shraddha, two beautiful marble temples containing the *Charan Peeth* (foot impressions) of Acharya ji and Mata ji. Thousands of men, women and children daily pour in prayers for bestowal of all round peace, prosperity and success in their life. Just in front of these temples, is the sacred tomb of Acharya ji and Mata ji made of sparkling granite stone, which draws enormous reverence from the people and are fully charged with celestial life consciousness.

The pious "Akhand Deep" (lamp) ignited by Acharya ji in 1926 is still lit at Shantikunj. In the light of this very lamp he conducted his twenty-four *Mahāpuraścharaṇas*. This Akhand Deep is a source of spiritual guidance for millions of men and women. Shantikunj has a splendid Yagyashala where *yagyas* are conducted daily morning for peace and prosperity for the whole world.

There is a temple devoted to the sacred Himalayas, where saints have lived for centuries and performed their penance. This temple is made in an oval shape and provides an ideal location for meditation in a calm, quiet and peaceful atmosphere. The temple of Himalaya is surrounded by lush green vegetation, and an exhibition of medicinal plants called Haritima Devalaya (temple of vegetation).

Shantikunj has elegant dispensaries of Aurveda, Homeopathy and Allopathy where qualified doctors render free service to patients. Medicines are also supplied free of cost on their prescription. They also render free advice for maintenance of sound health and improvement of natural immunity of the body system.

The Electronic Media Division of Shantikunj, which is playing a very important role in spreading the thoughts of Acharya ji to diverse sections of society. It has a basic audio-video production studio and it produces a large number of cassettes, and CDs for sale. Since video is a very powerful medium of mass communication, the media division has produced many films in different languages that convey the message of Acharya ji. These films are made on different topics like Acharya ji's spiritual discourses, important functions organized by Gayatri Pariwar, holistic health management, yoga and so on.

Shantikunj is daily visited by thousands of people from all walks of society. The spiritually purified and energetic ambience here attracts and impresses everyone who has ever visited this place. (See www.awgp.org for more information)

Brahmvarchas Research Institute:

Modern man could not be persuaded to accept the values of life propagated by ancient Rishis until and unless these were proved to be scientifically viable for the welfare of the individual and the society. Brahmvarchas Research Institute, the research centre of Shantikunj, Haridwar founded by Acharya ji in 1979 stands as a living example of how these ideas could be implemented and researched in the modern laboratories.

This center is dedicated to the integration of the modern and ancient sciences in a practical way motivated by the noble goal of health and happiness for all. Innovative scientific research in the ancient sciences aimed at grass root applications is being carried out here in collaboration with the relevant modern sciences. Major areas of research include Ayurveda and *Yagyopathy* (effective herbal inhalation therapy based on *yagya*), Complete Psychology, the Science of Mantra and its Therapeutic Applications, the Philosophy and Science of Yoga, *Sādhanā*, Gayatri Mantra, and the Science of Spirituality.

This center houses well equipped laboratories of haematology, biochemistry, neurophysiology, cardiology, phytochemistry, psychometry, *yagyopathy*, etc. Apart from its own team of doctors, engineers, scientists and philosophers, the center has live interaction with the hospital, Ayurvedic Pharmacy and Yoga labs of Shantikunj and with some of the hospitals and universities in and around Haridwar. Distinguished researchers, professors and other experts also visit the center regularly.

It has a rare collection of Himalayan herbs and medicinal samples prepared from the same after thorough experimental research. Several of the Ayurvedic medicines prepared here are in great demand as these have been found effective in the treatment of some otherwise incurable or advanced-stage diseases.

Tens of PhD degrees have been awarded by different universities in India based upon the research studies carried out here. Several more Ph D studies are also currently going on. The topics range from Vedic Cosmology, Yagyopathy,

Novel Herbal Therapies, Multiple Dimensions of Vedic Culture, to the effects of *Japa, Prāṇāyāma, Yoga-āsanas* and *Yagya* on Human Physiology and Psychology, etc. Brahmavarchas Institute also houses a unique library containing rare books and selected research journals to help in research studies.

Dev Sanskriti Vishwavidyalaya (Divine Culture University):

Almost five decades back, Acharya ji dreamt of a Dev Sanskriti Vishwa Vidyalaya (DSVV) that would infuse new life in the education system, and produce saplings for the Divine Era. India has had a tradition of famous Universities, like Nalanda & Takshshila of the Buddhist Age, which moulded good citizens for human values and global welfare. DSVV has been established to meet the pressing need to impart global education on scientific spirituality and life style. The university is bringing about ethical, moral and spiritual transformation of youths, and is producing specialists in various fields who are devoted nationalists. DSVV is playing a big role in imparting youth with excellent character, indomitable courage, firm determination, and intense love for labor. Recognized by the Uttaranchal Govt. and the UGC of India in 2002, this autonomous, self-funded university offers several undergraduate and postgraduate levels degree courses in Clinical Psychology, Yogic Science and Human Excellence, Indian Culture and Tourism, Value-based Journalism and Mass Communication, Applied Yoga Consciousness & Holistic Health. Excellent opportunities for self-learning and original research are available here in the above areas and also in Vedic Sciences, Indology and Oriental Studies.

To help wider sections of the society – especially the elderly people and those who may not have time to complete degree courses, the university offers some diploma level and certificate courses in — Yoga and human consciousness, Holistic Health Management, Theology, and Rural Management.

Admissions to all programs are based on qualifying entrance tests. Students get an opportunity to live in a larger family like ambience on the beautiful campus of the university surrounded by serene Himalayan beauty. Their schedule and method of teaching is designed to lay emphasis on cultivation of sensitivity and positive & altruistic attitudes, and self-analysis and self-learning. (See www.dsvv.org for more information).

Gayatri Tapobhumi, Mathura:

Gayatri Tapobhumi, located in Mathura, India was established in 1953 before the grand yagya described in previous chapter. The ever-flourishing seed of Gayatri Pariwar was sown here. This is a center for the mission's self-reliant education program and publication. The place consists of a magnificent temple of Gayatri, and several spiritual activities like daily *yagya*, mantra-writing, *japa*, meditation etc. go on regularly here. Several girls and boys live here in hostels and are provided free education. The Movement for the Reconstruction of the Era (*Yug Nirman Yojana*) was announced from this spiritually charged place itself. The mission owns two huge presses where all the magazines and thousands of books of the mission are published. There is a huge post office in the complex from where magazines of the mission are posted to all over the world.

Anwalkheda — Model Village

Anwalkheda village, the birthplace of Pandit Shriram Sharma Acharya, is located about 12 miles from Agra, India on Jalesar road. Mission runs an Intermediate College for girls and a hospital in this village. Anwalkheda is now being developed by Gayatri Pariwar as a model village under its Movement for the Creation of Ideal Villages (*Adarsh Gram Teerth Yojana*). Apart from being a place for pilgrimage for the devotees, this center is spreading the *Yug Nirman Mission's* rural development and social engineering projects.

Akhand Jyoti Sansthan:

Akhand Jyoti Sansthan is located in Mathura, India. This is the place where Acharya ji lived for about three decades, and completed most of his *Mahapurascharans,* participated in India's peaceful freedom struggle, and launched the *Yug Nirman Mission's* principal magazine "Akhand Jyoti" – the source of spreading the divine light of his thoughts. It is now the main center for the publication of "Akhand Jyoti", which along with its translated versions has over one million subscribers.

Expansion of the Mission:

The mission started by Acharya ji is now very wide spread. Gayatri Pariwar now has several million members who identify with the purpose behind the mission and willingly donate their time, energy and resources for the important cause. These are the people who have cleansed up their personal lives and ways of thinking following Acharya ji as their ideal. They have identified and removed personal bad attributes and refined their personalities by adopting virtues. Their efforts and devotion alone has lead to the expansion of Gayatri Pariwar to such an extent.

There are more than 4000 Shaktipeeths-Pragya Peeths (Centers of knowledge and divine cultural activities), 25000 Pragya Sansthans & 30,000 Swadhyaya Mandals (self-study groups) of the mission in all parts of India. All members of Gayatri Pariwar practise *upāsanā* of Gayatri every day. This combined meditative prayer accounts for about 1.40 billion chants of the Gayatri Mantra a day. There is no account of collective *sādhanā* of this magnitude anywhere in world's history. There is a firm belief among all members of this Pariwar that this effort of theirs would cleanse up the evil in peoples' minds and create an environment conducive to the birth of a new era.

Gayatri Yagya was a medium chosen by Acharya ji for spreading noble thoughts for the new era. He explained to everyone that Gayatri symbolizes righteous way of thinking and *yagya* symbolizes putting noble ideas into action. Hundreds-of-thousands of these *yagyas* have been conducted now all over the country and have spread Acharya ji's message to masses. Yug Nirman meets have been conducted in large numbers to motivate people to work towards self-development, development of family and then development of the society. Through these meets people have been awakened to fight against evil tendencies, malpractices, and illogical customs and traditions prevalent in society. Innumerable people have refined their thoughts and set aside evil-mindedness in front of sacred fire of *yagya* and have adopted virtuous life styles.

Education of masses and spreading awareness has been a very important task taken up by the mission. In addition to teaching self-development, the mission has educated people about how to build happy families and create heavenly atmosphere at home. For this, people have been taught to inculcate the five-fold virtues of industriousness, prudent expenditure, orderliness, politeness and cooperation in the nature and behavior of every member of family. Well-cultured families have always been a source of refined individuals; they are like mines that produce jewels. Families form the all-important links between an individual and society. Yug Nirman mission has thoughtfully focused its attention to creating healthy and cultured families, which would act as breeding grounds for worthy citizens. Never before has any other movement focused on this important issue in a practical and organized manner.

The next focus of Yug Nirman mission has been the development of society. One of the important programmes that the mission has taken up is to put an end to the custom of extravagant marriages. The mission has put intense efforts to curb this evil through mass movement and has instated the custom of simple marriages and mass marriages. Ideal marriages are conducted in Shantikunj and all its centres free of cost and innumerable such marriages have been conducted till date. Mission has strongly advocated against dowry system also in these ideal marriages.

The struggle against discrimination based upon castes and social orders has been another focus of the mission. It has tried to integrate several different communities and join them into nationalistic way of thinking.

There are several evil customs and practices prevalent in society. The mission has launched a massive movement against bad practices like extravagant feasts in memory of the dead, beggary, *pardā* (veil) custom, child marriages, excess expenditure on jewelry and fashion, intoxication etc. People have been convinced with logical reasoning to restrict their families to maximum two offspring only.

The mission has trained many volunteers for important programmes like adult education and running free-of-cost yoga centers for good health. A large number of people have been trained to plant and look after trees, and cultivate vegetable and herbal gardens in their localities.

Message of this grand plan has been spread to all sections of the society through music and songs, speeches, mission's magazines, fortnightly news magazines, religious functions, and with the help of videos, etc. Mission has taken great care to spread its message to people of Indian origin residing in other countries as well. It has motivated immigrant people to keep their Indian traditions and language alive on foreign soil. The mission's centers are now located in over 70 countries around the globe which try to bring people together and organize their activities for creative endeavors.

To encourage activities of the mission at all levels several workers are actively involved within and outside the country. This has become possible by rejuvenating the tradition of Vanprastha (*Vānsprastha*) Ashram. Earlier householders and Brahmins used to devote themselves for social service in their neighborhood, while senior people who took up Vanprastha, took up service in much wider areas. Yug Nirman mission has built and trained social workers of all ages and sections of society to spread its message in the whole world. It has managed to bring in its fold several talented individuals and has encouraged them to devote their energies for the important social causes.

Additional Reading:

1. Reviving The Vedifc Culture of Yagya. (Translation of Hindi book *'Hamara Yagya Abhiyan'* by Dr. Pranav Pandya). Publ. Shri Vedmata Gayatri Trust Shantikunj, Haridwar. 3rd Print 2005.

2. *Mahāpuraścaraṇa*: Unique Spiritual Experiment on Collective Consciousness. (Translation of the Hindi book *'Yug Sandhi Mahāpuraścaraṇa'* by Dr. Pranav Pandya). Publ. Shri Vedmata Gayatri Trust Shantikunj, Haridwar. 3rd Print 2005.

Evolutionary Force of Time-Spirit has Triggered the Waves of a Grand Change | 8

The vicissitudinous tides of time have posed two alarming challenges today: one, the need to eradicate the horrifying smog of the risks of total devastation of the world; and, two, creation of a new world order for a bright, progressive and happy future. These are Herculean tasks that may be likened to charring the giant kingdom of Ravana into ashes and simultaneously establishing *"Rāma-Rājya"* – the ideal empire of Lord Ram.

Threats to Life on the Earth:

The prevailing circumstances on the global scenario indicate strong possibilities of hazardous conflicts and calamities, prominent among these are the threats of nuclear, biological and (variants of) star wars and another world war. If either of these materializes, it will lead to total extinction of the civilization and will also extinguish the chances of existence of life on this planet forever. Not only that! It might even destroy the very existence of our lovely planet and explode it into pieces like the debris of the tiny stars devastated after collision, which continues to revolve between the Mars and Jupiter. The danger of nuclear, biological or chemical warfare is more terrifying than all the combined demonic powers narrated in mythology. Even a thought of its likelihood would send shivers in the minds of anyone who knows the dreaded powers of these devilish tools. The sword of doom's day seems to be hanging above every head. Who knows when the earth might be exploded into a comet of toxic smoke? The pathetic aftermaths of nuclear attacks on Hiroshima, Nagasaki and the state of affairs post wars in the gulf are sufficient to make us imagine the magnitude and nature of the hazards we are living with, noting especially the multifold sophistication and expansion of strategic weapons technology every day.

Another scarecrow that has spread its dark wings on the earth is environmental pollution. The blind race of materialistic gains and uncontrolled mushrooming of industries has proved suicidal in many respects. The toxic smoke of the factories and industrial waste has poisoned the air, water and soil. In the urbanized or industrially developed areas, we can't even breathe fresh air. Ponds, rivers and even seawater are polluted. Global warming generated by atmospheric pollution has further augmented the scarcity of water for drinking and irrigation and compounded the negative effects. Use of chemical fertilizers, synthesized seeds and pesticides has ruined the fertility of soil and mutated the agricultural products. Detection of pesticides, carcinogens and other harmful chemicals in food grains, vegetables and fruits has become a common observation; at times these are even found much above the high-risk levels. Unchecked exploitation of geological resources has squeezed out the treasures of oil, petroleum and rich varieties of minerals beneath the earth on the one hand and also enhanced the propensity of earthquakes in several parts of the world on the other.

The third giant menace waiting to gulp us all is that of untoward radiations. As though the ultraviolet and other harmful radiations of the sun reaching us due to depletion of the ozone layer were not enough to increase our panic, our follies seem to 'assure' us of more tragic and painful suffering! The ever rising research and development activities in the field of nuclear energy – for production of the atomic bombs and generation of thermal electricity have, despite the much acclaimed safety norms, increased the radio-active radiations in earth's atmosphere beyond the safe limits. This is a virtual invitation to diseases like cancer and debilitating disabilities and genetic aberrations of many kinds. We the grownups, we the intellectuals, the scientists, technologists, industrialists, developers, or administrators of today appear headed to creating a hell for our future generations. Instead of a rise in prosperity and happiness, we seem to be pushing our world to unprecedented pain and suffering, disabilities and adversity of Nature.

On the fourth front there is the dragon of population explosion! Just imagine, the world population was only 150 millions about two thousands years ago. With a growth rate like compounded interest we have now crossed the figure of 6000 millions! If this cyclonic trend continues, within less than half a century we will be more than 10,000 millions!! It is impossible to fulfill the basic necessities like fresh air, water, food, housing, education, medical support and transportation for such a huge crowd. Economic and developmental growth would not be able to meet the demands imposed by the high fertility rate of human population. Even theoretically, no expert has been able to provide any magic idea or model in this regard. What will happen when the roads will be all the time flooded with vehicles and pedestrians? Will anybody be able to walk or move in any direction without crushing a few fellow beings? Like the hoards of locust, people would be virtually compelled to suicides on large scale. So even if one were able to survive the lethal pollution, radioactivity, and hunger, etc, he would die of suffocation or be mashed in the crowds rushing from all directions.

Ironically, none of the above is a natural calamity. These are all man-made blunders. In spite of the savants being aware of the acute dimensions of the problems, and in spite of brainstorming discussions and grand projects at national and international levels, there appears no satisfactory and feasible solution in sight. The hopes of rescue from the 'death-valley' remain grim. Why is it so? Why the modern world, so well-equipped with super-powers of science and technology, intellectual ascent and liberty of thoughts has trapped itself in the vicious cycle of suicidal follies, that too in the blossoming spring of its civilization and materialistic prosperity? In simplest terms the root cause is our ignorance and negligence of the soul. This indifference and disrespect towards the real self has also strengthened the nearest and mightiest but hidden enemy of mankind, which is — decline in moral values.

Fallen moral values and selfish attitudes have converted today's man into an intelligent beast, a wealth-producing machine, and even into a demon in human form. Human values like goodwill, love, generosity, altruistic feelings, and sacrifice have become meaningless and obsolete in today's society at large. Integrity of character, sacrifice for ideals sound imaginary to most people or have become the subject matters of fun and ridicule. Sensitivity of human heart is overshadowed by arrogance and avarice; thirst for sensual pleasure and blind race for superficial success, shortsighted ambitions and mean aims have suppressed all moral instincts and waned all memories of great characters. Cultural decline and crisis of faith is at its peak. In short, despite immensity of glittering resources we are shallow in personality. We are falling down along a slippery path in terms of real dignity. Our materialistic progress has reached sky high but the roots and fruits of progress have gone rotten. The gigantic skeleton of our development has drifted off from its foundation; it would fall any time and dump us in the ditch of darkness forever.

Each one of the above-described five threats is frightening and is sufficient to challenge our existence on the earth. How difficult it would be to tackle their joint impact should be obvious to anyone who thinks. Looking at the gravity of the threats and reviewing what the preventive and remedial efforts have been made so far by the governments and social organizations across the globe, it is apparent that much more is essential to be done on war footing. Considering the emergency of the situation and realizing the root of the problems, we need to harness the potential of the field of spirituality.

Spiritual Experiment to Counter the Threats:

The demon Vrattasur would not have been destroyed if Indra's *vraj* (divine weapon) were not used. And what made this *vraj* so powerful? It was made up of the bones of *rishi*

Dadhichi, which he voluntarily donated to save the world. It was the spiritual energy of the *rishi* that had made his bones so special. The dimension of the 'Vrattasur' today is manifold and much more gigantic. One *vraj* alone would not suffice to defeat it. Today, we require the elevated spiritual force, which is immense like the cosmic vibrations generated by evolutionary impulse (*Mahākālī Śakti*) of the Omnipotent. This requires devout *sādhanās* in the high realms of supreme consciousness force. Pandit Shriram Sharma Acharya ji has endeavored this epochal experiment in his subtle and astral bodies along with angelic *rishis* present in invisible forms in the intractable core of the Himalayas.

This unique experiment had commenced in 1984 with his *"Sukṣmīkaraṇa Sādhanā"* which has continued with greater force[1 & 2] since he voluntarily left the physical body in 1990. In his physical body as well, the life of this seer-sage, spiritual scientist par excellence had been a living monument of *tapa-sādhanās* of great intensity including twenty-four *Gāyatrī Mahāpuraścharaṇas* for twenty-four years. He also pioneered mass-awakening and spiritual upliftment of the masses from all walks of life through the grass-root programs of social welfare, revolution of thoughts and dissemination of spiritual knowledge in scientific light. The seeds sown by him are fructifying with millions of people participating in the *"Yug Nirman"* mission of the Gayatri Pariwar propounded by him.

His unique spiritual experiment has churned and purified the sublime environment of life, consequences of which are clearly seen as the dawn of a golden future by the *yogis* and *sādhakas* who can perceive the horizons beyond the space and time limits. Rise in people's curiosity and inclination towards spirituality, expansion in the reach of dedicated schools and organizations of *yoga* and spirituality to distant corners of the globe, and growing popularity of the constructive programs of these institutions is a definite indication of a positive change that we cannot ignore. This also signals that the smog of 'crisis of faith' is somewhat diminishing, and gradually the sunrise of moral upliftment will also appear in the clear sky.

The changes in the subtle ambience will materialize in entirety if we also put in our best efforts on what pertains to our immediate duties for the betterment of our world. There are five principal fronts where the current trends need to be set right; it is an exercise of rotating back the wrong side down and bringing the right side at the top. It will require reformative as well as reconstructive strives to rectify the errors and to accelerate the righteous efforts of ploughing, irrigating and cultivating the world-garden. This would turn a barren land, a stretch of filthy mire, into a green flourishing belt, a fragrant farm of sandalwood. Each of these fronts is like a stout pillar on which the architecture of the society, the nation, the world, resides. These are the five nuclei of power that shape the present and future of the people. It is up to the people to channelize these powerful streams. These five perennial resources are – (i) Government; (ii) Religion; (iii) Economy; (iv) Knowledge and (v) Talents.

(i) Government:

Government or ruling regime of a nation holds the key to its security, foreign affairs and major policy decisions. All resources and revenues of the country are mobilized under direct or indirect control of the government. It is a pity that a somewhat destructive and insensitive line of thoughts is dominating the approaches of most rulers. Advancement of strategic gadgets, secret intelligence and preparations for high-tech war are their prime concerns. Blame it on the system as a whole, cold war culture, conservative approach of some 'superpower countries', or religious fanaticism, the fact remains that most of the governments, due to whatever reasons they might try to justify, are responsible for fuming the human resources, financial, intellectual, scientific and technological powers and creative talents of their nations in the fire of defense-expenditures. It is not hidden from anyone that most of the countrymen – the common people are against wars and want to live peaceful and progressive life. Why then, there is a threat of war, or occurrence of war? Does the military on its own initiates it at random? Certainly not! We all know that it is their 'high commands', the handful of rulers – the policy makers, the decision makers, whose 'vision' and orders make all the difference. The loggerhead violent bullfight seriously injures and even kills the bulls and also ruins the plants and vegetation around. The battle of the 'heads' of the nations is more intense. It harms their own country more than the enemy's.

Even if half the energy and other resources engaged for violence and destruction could be used wisely for constructive purposes, by now the malnutrition, poverty, unemployment, illiteracy, would have been eradicated from this world. It would have also helped improvement of people's health control over criminal mentality and activities. If there is positive transformation at the top (government, leading forces), amelioration of the whole system won't be difficult. Farsighted wisdom, goodwill and righteous actions of rulers and leaders can bring revolutionary changes without any 'revolution' and accelerate the chances of golden future.

(ii) Religion:

The second foundational pillar of the human society is religion. The real meaning of religion is – linkage of consciousness with nobility; implanting magnanimity and human values in people's hearts and minds; righteous orientation of thoughts, emotions and actions. Illusory doctrines and fundamentalist impositions in the name of religion or faith are mere offshoots of prejudiced communalism propagated by the few so-called 'religious leaders' or 'extremist philosophers' who exploit the simplicity and emotional softness of innocent peoples. Unfortunately, since several hundred years, these distortions have overshadowed the spirit and light of religion. This sheath needs to be peeled off at the earliest so that the immense power of spirituality could be used for self-awakening and moral elevation of the masses. This can't be achieved simply by sacraments, grand ceremonial gathering, festivals, devotional songs or prayer meetings. Dissemination of the true meaning and purpose of religion and ethics of humanity can be executed by enlightening writings, discourses, art, culture, and altruistic deeds.

Literature, performing art, films, and above all, the media play a crucial role in moulding the tendencies of the masses. However, in the modern times, the web of consumerism and commercialization has entrapped everything so much that grabbing profit and power by easy encashment of beastly instincts and passions and by all (fair or unfair) means appears to have generally become the motto of success for the high flying masters of these fields. The corruption of these intense modes of wide-reach among the masses is responsible, to a significant extent, for declining standards of people's taste and for moral devolution of the society. The most sensitive and intense root of debauching adulteration of people's tendencies and consequent mushrooming of social crimes, terrors, addictions, perversion of youths, ethical anarchy, etc has to be 'cured' on war-footing. It is urgent like controlling the engine that has gone off the track and is about to fall in a ditch with the entire train. Rectification on this front and expansion of the light of religion should go hand in hand.

(iii) Economy:

The third vertebra of the spinal cord of our civilization is money-power – strong economy or financial resources. Indeed wealth is the most prominent source of materialistic development. From acquisition of bare minimum necessities of survival and essential worldly requirements, to glittering enterprises, gorgeous status, expansion of business and estate, and industrial growth, everything needs finance. Wealth could be used thoughtfully towards fulfilling essential requirements, raising family, contributing for social welfare, supporting philanthropic projects, rural development, setting up small or large-scale industries, generating employments, etc. But it can also be spent on lavish life-style, excessive possession of luxuries, sensual pleasures and passions and untoward addictions. Money can be stolen or grabbed by deceiving and extortion. But it can also be generated by industrious efforts, sharp business skills, sincerity and efficient management. And it can be put in use for constructive projects of strengthening the economic status of the society, of the nation, and thus directly or indirectly contributing to the prosperity of the world.

What we see currently is partly a mixed scenario on the front of wealth generation and utilization. However, dishonesty, shrewdness, corruption and selfish possessions are somewhat predominant on this front too.

Things won't remain the same for long! Nature will set the clock right very soon on this relatively more visible and worldly front. As we all are experiencing, lavish food and luxurious life-style brings along varieties of psychosomatic disorders and weaknesses in return. Tensions and stresses also grow in proportion with thirst for money, ambitions of rapid accumulation of wealth, fast expansion of business, etc. The penalties are going to be stricter in the coming years. Moreover, those exploited or oppressed would not keep quiet any more. There are forums and organizations, which, for whatever vested interests or goodwill, often come forward to help the labors and others being exploited. Such efforts are going to gear up with fairness in fight for justice.

Global economy has become a reality today; for it to flourish further, all disparities and partisan approaches ought to vanish. Whether one believes it or not, the coming decades will witness a more balanced distribution of capital, cooperation and non-hierarchical collaboration between workers and owners. No wise man or woman would snatch or hold excessive wealth or worldly resources without investing them towards expansion of prosperity of many others. Those who will continue to stock hoards of riches for selfish means and passions will face the music. Nature and the society will teach them a good lesson in not too distant future. Those having wealth and also the wisdom and vision of the future will give due consideration to needs of the hour and orient their financial-planning and resources towards philanthropy and constructive projects of socio-economic development and welfare of more and more needy people. They will be the worthy contributors to the making of a prosperous world. Those who would grab wealth for narrow selfish purposes and pleasures will have nothing but repentance to own in the end.

(iv) **Knowledge:**

We are all aware that knowledge is the most powerful source of progress on the materialist and intellectual fronts. Ascent of our civilization and social development would not have taken place without knowledge. The past millennium has witnessed intellectual evolution that has propelled us in the present 'age of knowledge'. However, much more remains to be done. So far, our knowledge has largely remained confined to 'understanding of some facets of Nature' and 'information of the happenings in the world'.

Our learning or 'knowledge acquisition' is driven by our education system. School and university education has steered its dissemination in a formal way (*śikṣā*) as per the trends of development and requirements of the society. The expansion of media and advancement of communication technology have led to a virtual explosion of information. But how much of that is really useful for refinement of personality? Knowledge of findings of natural and social sciences, information and contemporary analysis of the local and global events is no doubt essential for progress on the external domains of life. But what about the absolute knowledge (*vidyā*), which enlightens the inner self, inculcates moral values and acquaints us with the purpose and grandeur of our lives? Is it only a subject matter of mystic philosophy or abstract religion? No, *vidyā* is as vital to our happy progress as *śikṣā*. It is *vidyā* that makes us, not only thinking 'machines', skilled professionals, and eminent scholars, but also sensitive and responsible citizens, good human beings and illumined great personalities. It is crucial for lasting happiness of the individuals and the society.

Today, as we find in India and in most of the developing or underdeveloped countries, education sector, even at the level of *śikṣā* alone has been in bad shape. Dependence on government alone for free or less-expensive education is not going to achieve the needful in the countries where more than half the population is illiterate. Every learned fellow, every literate citizen will have to bear his/her share of responsibility to educate others around him, to at least enable them read, write and be inspired to learn more. The ongoing efforts of night schools, adult education, informal and vocational education – including small scale, village and domestic industries need to be mobilized and expanded manifold along with education of hygiene, preventive medicines, behavioral psychology, communication, and mass awareness against blind customs and superstitions. Moral education, value-based development, cultivation of positive, eco-friendly and cooperating approach for everybody's welfare should be an integral part of all educational projects. It sounds too ambitious today. But we are to strive for it our level best, because today's world is moving along a thin and sharp edge. Our grand civilization, our very existence may slip anytime unless we create strong support on both sides. For this we will have to look forward in all directions, realize the necessities of tomorrow and exert our duties on every front of education and acquisition and augmentation of knowledge with enlightenment.

The new phase of evolution beyond intellect has just begun and is going to embrace the horizons of thoughts, emotions and inner sentiments. Awakened savants are going to disseminate *vidyā* in all walks of life. Education system and learning is now going to serve the real purpose of knowledge-expansion via a confluence of *śikṣā* and *vidyā*.

(V) Talents:

The fifth vital source for creation of brighter future is — channelization of talents and creative potentials. The talents of scientists, engineers, doctors, writers, journalists, lawyers, poets, singers, musicians, artists, etc are indeed distinct. They owe greater responsibility in developing, maintaining and beautifying this world. This moral obligation and goodwill of talented individuals was the secret of unparalleled development of science, arts and culture in ancient India. Talents if devoted to altruistic duties and noble deeds are like *rishis*, who are worthy of being revered like angels.

Unfortunately, large fraction of this elite section of the human society seems to have forgotten its duties or have preferred selfish gains, money and other favors in lieu of haute ethics of their own professions! If it were not so, how could the production of dreaded high-tech weapons be possible? How could there be injustice in the courts-of-law? How could the media be prejudiced? How could it allow advertisement and propagation of obscenity? Why art and literature would have been supporting eroticism, animosity and violence? Why would talented orators be misleading the masses for vested interests?

Indeed eminent talents can influence the mentality of the masses and drive it towards the right or the wrong. The argument of filmmakers, press, writers, etc that they have to go as per people's taste and social trend carries little weightage noting that mob-psychology does not have any originality. Most people simply follow what has been hyped or repeated before them exploiting their weaknesses. Scientists, engineers, doctors and other professionals, intellectuals and talented personalities hold the key to economic development. Why don't they join hands and come forward to compel the governments or rulers to rectify the wrongs? Why can't the artists, actors and the media show some courage, sacrifice some of their quick-benefits and devote their time and skills to mold the interests of the masses towards non-beastly tendencies, positive attitude and constructive activities? Why don't they be vigilant and support the organizations and people that are genuinely working for social-upliftment? Why don't they compete to inspire people for value-based life-style?

It would need only a nudge of spiritual force, a flash of inner light to enable them to do all that which is ideally expected of them by virtue of their talents and creative potentials. Recall the examples of Valmiki, Angulimal, Bilvamangal, Tulsidas, Amrapali and King Ashoka whose course of life was reverted downside-up in no time by some incidents of being inspired by the *rishis* or some biting experiences that shook their inner selves.

Even tiny straws of dry grass and dust particles rise up to sky-heights in the immense storm of a Hurricane. Then just imagine the consequences of more intense spiritual cyclones! They can convert dullness into alacrity, insanity into sagacity and miraculously transform the flow of time and circumstances beyond any bounds. One doesn't have to go too far to search for evidences! Just turn the pages of our recent history. It was not a mere coincidence that a galaxy of great leaders like Mahatma Gandhi, Nehru, Bose, Tilak, Bhagat Singh, etc appeared in a specific period of Indian History for the same purpose. The silent spiritual *sādhanā* experiments of Sri Aurobindo and Maharshi Raman and the consequent rise, the gigantic expansion and triumph of the wave of non-violent freedom-movement of India are testimony to the impact of sublime ambience.

This time the force of the spiritual cyclone is going to be far more strong and widespread. It is generated by the epochal *sūkṣmīkaraṇa sādhanā* of the seer-sage Taponishtha

Vedmurthy Pandit Shriram Sharma Acharya. Like the five *Virabhadras* of Lord Shiva the five fold currents of its spiritual storm will ruin the five dragon-arms that have threatened the existence of life on this planet. At the same time, the evolutionary impulse of spirituality sparked by this *sādhanā* will inspire the five principal sources of erecting the golden era of happy, prosperous and virtuous life.

Additional Reading/ References:

1 & 2. *Sukśmīkaraṇa aur Ujjaval Bhavishya ka Avatarana* (*Satyug Ki Vāpasī*). – 1 & 2. Pandit Shriram Sharma Acharya Samagra Vangmaya Vols. 28 & 29, Akhand Jyoti Sansthan, Mathura (India), 1995.

3.   Great Moments of Change. (2nd Ed.) Yugantariya Chetna Press, Haridwar, 2000.

Renaissance of Spirituality
Promises of Golden Future

9

On a foggy or cloudy day, or at the time of eclipse, even the daytime appears dark. But this darkness is only temporary. Brilliance of sunlight begins to shine with golden glow as soon as the smog is cleared or the shadow of eclipse shifts. The light of pure wisdom and sagacious acumen seems to have been blocked these days by a thick haze of illusions, superficiality, ostentations (hypocrisy), and widespread fallacious tendencies of quick-gains by whatever means. Nevertheless, the silver line of hope is that nothing is permanent in this world. The mist of ignorance and confusion that has pervaded the field of spirituality and religion is also going to be cleared soon.

The "Age of Truth" of the prehistoric times is going to revive in the future. In the post Vedic era, in mainly the medieval and the present times, humanity has suffered all round decline and degradation of the value-systems, and consequent attack of untoward tendencies, ignorance and distortions. This attack was hidden but akin to the attack of locusts and other pests, who arrive in huge groups, spread like a wide, thick sheet on the blossoming crop and ruin it in no time. Similar attack has occurred in the field of spiritual disciplines in this dark phase of several thousands of years. But thanks to the self-organizing system of Nature, the roots of spirituality remained alive in the pure minds and hearts of the great saints and sages. The long years of persistent endeavors of these elevated souls have ploughed and prepared the grounds for renaissance of spirituality to its original dignity.

The onset of new millennium may also be viewed as dawn of the new phase of change of an era. This is the phase of renovation, resurrection and reconstruction. New, luminous edifice of ancient culture is going to be built on its long forgotten and buried foundations. The architecture of new era will be a robust, glittering replica of its glorious past and will be erected by collective efforts of millions of awakened souls. The winds of new joy and enthusiasm have begun to blow in the subtle horizons to rejuvenate our energies for this unprecedented task. Human civilization in its ascent has witnessed culmination of intellectual evolution in the modern times. Now it will undergo mental, emotional, and spiritual evolution.

Spiritual evolution is not anything occult or imaginary. As we have discussed earlier, spirituality is not magic, mystery, or metaphysical faculty of spirits in the realms of life after death. Neither does it emanate from or deal with any religious doctrine or sacramental practice. Contrary to common beliefs and misconceptions, spirituality is a science. It is a science of self-awakening, refinement and virtuous transmutation of personality. It is a process of progress of individuals and the society as a whole that ensures auspicious welfare and well-being of all.

The onset of new millennium lies at the juncture of two eras. These are the years of epochal changes. Several futurologists have predicted that the 21st century would be full of devastating wars, natural disasters, energy crises and diseases, etc. Scientific analyses based on projected consumption rates and availability of natural resources, risks of population explosion, environmental pollution, ecosystem imbalance, unemployment, etc also indicate similarly. But only those having extraordinary acumen can see that the spiritually empowered souls, in the visible or sublime forms are engaged in the grand churning that would stir out and throw away the poison and fetch in the elixir. Spiritual saints and sagacious visionaries like *Yugrishi* Pandit Shriram Sharma Acharya have therefore assured that renaissance of spirituality and its constructive integration with science[1] would transform the prevailing circumstances and revert the cycle of declining human culture towards positive growth with possibilities of farsighted reconstruction and upliftment on all fronts of life. The natural calamities, wars etc will be there in the early decades of this new era but will be checked from making global impact. Gradually, the intensity of negativity will cease and the change in the subtle world will get more and more visible in the manifested world (the world we live in) with new light of brighter tomorrow[2, 3].

The amazing scientific progress in transportation, aviation and communication technology have virtually converted the world into a global village. Mutual dependence in trade and economics has also brought the nations closer, in a single fold. The same is going to happen in the political scenario as well. Therefore the problems of the world should not be addressed only locally or regionally, there ought to be global solutions, which should also be implemented globally at one shot rather than being tried out individually and at remote levels. As we all know, applying medicinal ointments on the acnes of smallpox cannot cure the disease. Blood-purification or elimination of the virus from the patient's body by timely immune response is an essential remedy in this case. Killing them one by one cannot check excessive growth of flies and mosquitoes. We need to cleanse the entire colony and even neighboring localities to get rid of these insects and likely epidemic diseases. These familiar examples illustrate that the best approach to tackling the challenges daring the world today would be – to face and solve them collectively. The entire world should be viewed like one large nation, like a global family, which is united by the relation of humanity. The collective potential of human society is immense enough to root out the gamut of unsocial, terrorist and all sorts of negative elements in no time and also to resolve the plethora of other problems rising in different parts of the world. There is no challenge, howsoever gigantic that might appear today, which cannot be conquered by the immense force of collective consciousness.

The end of 20th century and the initial decades of the 21st will witness horrifying natural calamities together with the grand tug-of-war between the evil and the good, collision between conflicting philosophies of life, between rival cultures, etc. But at the same time, there will also be gradual strengthening and augmenting of cooperation between the constructive efforts of welfare and farsighted organization of liberal systems. This positive development will accelerate at an increasing pace with every year of the new millennium. The blueprint of the golden future ahead was clear in the clairvoyance and precognition of the *rishis* of our times, like Pandit Shriram Sharma Acharya way back in the 1920s. He and elevated souls like him have also contributed their intense *tapa – sādhanā* to awaken collective consciousness and to create the necessary ambience for the dawn of the golden era by 2020+.

The unique feature of the new world order will be: integration of modern science and spirituality and assimilation of spiritual values in socio cultural, economic, and political developments. Every field of life will be illumined by pure radiance of spirituality. The principles of *vasudhaiva kutumbakaṁ* (entire world is like a family) and *ātmavat sarvabhūteṣu* (everyone is like one's own self) will materialize in reality in this very world. Unity and convergence will be the watchwords of all ideologies and humanity will be the predominant religion[2, 3].

Interdependence and cooperation at the economical, technological, educational and socio-political levels will be so extensive that the domestic as well as international administrative bodies will function like waves in a global ocean. Where will then be a place for wars? The huge resources spent in national security and defense-technologies will then be diverted for upliftment and well-being of the masses. Mobilization of talents for down-to-earth projects and inclination of most people for disciplined and simple life-style would serve a great deal in alleviating the projected crises on the crucial fronts of energy, environment and health.

Disparity in use of land will be removed and people from crowded regions will be free to inhabit more spacious places beyond any constraints of national borders. By then, Nature would have taught substantial lessons to mankind, so the accumulation and luxurious consumption of wealth and power will be waned out from people's life. Human society would have experienced the joy and gains of giving and helping others, so no one would like to commit the mistake of selfish possession any more. Equality among people without any barrier of race, creed, gender, socio-economic status, etc, will no longer be a utopian concept. Every man and woman will then enjoy equal rights and opportunities and live a happy and duty-bound life. Indeed one feels most happy in sharing and distributing whatever he has among all the loved ones. All this will be a natural consequence of spiritual outlook that induces a feeling of oneness with all beings.

Communication technology has already bridged the gaps due to geographical distances. Adding to this, Information Technology has virtually removed the barriers of languages, and accelerated the circulation of literature and transmission of information by virtually connecting people across the globe via the Internet. This has enabled all to access the same information at the same time, know each other's culture, literature and society more closely, and letting them freely chat and interact with practically everyone, everywhere! With enhanced prudence and matured attitude of people in the coming decades, we shall see redundancies, distortions, and misuses of the world-wide-web and satellite links being replaced by intelligent and constructive uses of these amazing gifts of science and technology to impart expertise and experiences and to acquire and expand knowledge.

The history of human civilization has witnessed numerous revolutions of varied intensities that have turned the trends of life and changed the shape of the world in specific periods. These include industrial revolution, communist or labour revolution, anti-imperialism or pro-democracy revolutions, social revolution, and intellectual, scientific and technological revolutions. An unprecedented revolution in the 21st century will now transform this era. It will be a revolution of thoughts, emotions and values. It will uproot the vices, untoward tendencies, disparities and conflicts, and destroy the foundations of all fallacies and debouches. It will turn the wrongs upside down and set everything right, worth the dignity of human life. Indeed, it will be a spiritual revolution.

It was the evolutionary impulse of the Omnipotent Consciousness Force (*Brahm*) that created this amazing universe and manifestation of countless life forms on the planets like our earth. Just imagine the grandeur of the transformation of the fireball earth into the modern world flourishing with amazing high-tech gadgets that have carried its 'message' to the other planets and stars beyond the solar system! This is only a glimpse of the power of the Consciousness Force hidden in a human being. We may not be aware, but the evolution of consciousness continues now as ever and would lead to divine ascent in a compatible spiritual ambience. The present phase of our lives has bestowed this exceptional opportunity of spiritual transmutation.

The spiritual revolution we are referring to is inspired and backed by sublime divine powers. They will invisibly motivate and guide the awakened souls in all walks of life to participate in this epochal revolution. Irrespective of whether they know it or not, whether they want it or not, all those having a compassionate heart and all those who care or at least think to save human values, to save the ecosystem and the future of the world, will feel some inexplicable inner urge to change themselves, to have farsighted sensitivity, to adopt spirituality and spread its light among those around them. If they continue to neglect it, the thrust of Nature will compel them to awaken. The waves of revolutionary changes will gradually embrace every one. The elevated souls who would lead this reform on the visible fronts have already arrived and are playing or going to play their key roles. The necessary ambience for this unique transition has already been created in the subtle world. The seeds are sown and saplings have also begun to sprout. They would gradually grow into trees and there will be a paradise of blossoming gardens on this land. The new revolution will eventually erect heavens on the earth.

An evidential example of how this revolution would progress, can be seen at a miniature level in the extraordinary achievements of the Yug Nirman Mission propounded by *Yugrishi* Pandit Shriram Sharma Acharya. In the earlier Chapters of this book, we have seen a brief outline of the life and works of this sagacious saint (*rishi*) of our times, who pioneered renaissance of scientific spirituality and established working models of the institutions developed in its light in the form of Shantikunj at Haridwar, Brahmvarchas Research Center at Haridwar, Gayatri Tapobhumi at Mathura and numerous allied organizations and centers of the Gayatri

Pariwar. Recent expansions of this mission include the first of its kind Dev Sanskriti University (DSVV) at Haridwar. What has been told and known about this angelic personality so far is only a tip of the iceberg. He kept himself away from publicity and never exposed his supernatural powers, as it would have only made people curious about his supernorm.al or magical personality and crazy for taking his blessings. This would have added to the misconceptions about spirituality as dealing with a mysterious or occult world. He believed, experimented and proved that spirituality is a science.

His life and works are paragons of how the devout endeavors of *tapa* and *yoga-sādhanās* are possible in ordinary life along with praiseworthy fulfillment of familial and social responsibilities. His time-tested foretells, conveyed through his logical interpretations and implications[4] affirm that the spiritual revolution and dawn of the superconsciousness force as envisaged by him and spiritual saints of his caliber is going to be a reality in this very world.

Many of those who have had the opportunity to meet, interact and be guided by spirituality enlightened personalities must have realized that spirituality is certainly a science of elevated psychology and enlightened emotions, a science of evolution of consciousness, a science of awakening divinity hidden in our inner selves. It is our ardent responsibility and also the urgent need of our times to deracinate all prejudices, misconceptions, and inhibitions, to eliminate all distortions, and to rectify all deformations and delusive convictions about spirituality. Mingling religion with communalism, insane beliefs and traditions and confusing spirituality with esoteric hallucinations, metaphysical imaginations, some sort of black magic, and obscure notions of life after death, ghosts, etc, has been a curse on human society. It has deprived us of benefiting from the most precious and most powerful source of illumined progress towards unlimited peace, prosperity and unalloyed joy an ' instead, has driven us and our mighty science and intellectual civilization to a wrong, slippery path. Its time all of us who can think liberally – independently of popular trend and intellectual bias, should learn, adopt and disseminate the true meaning and purpose of spirituality in new scientific light.

References:

1. *Vigyāna aur Adhyātma Paraspar Pūraka.* Pandit Shriram Sharma Acharya Samagra Vangmaya Vol. 23, Akhand Jyoti Sansthan, Mathura (India), 1995.

2. *Yug Parivartan: Kaise aur Kaba?* Pandit Shriram Sharma Acharya Samagra Vangmaya Vol. 27, Akhand Jyoti Sansthan, Mathura (India), 1995.

3. 21st Century — Dawn of the Era of Divine Descent on Earth. Yugantariya Chetna Press, Haridwar, 2003.

4. A Glimpse of the Golden Future – As Foretold by Pandit Shriram Sharma Acharya. Shri Vedmata Gayatri Trust Shantikunj, Haridwara 2006. ISBN: 81-8255-014-9

Glossary of Sanskrit Words Used in This Book:

Anuṣṭhāna: Determined ascetic endeavor aimed at noble spiritual purpose.

Japa: Continuous rhythmic enunciation or chanting

Mahāpuraścharaṇa: A grand *puraścaraṇa*. (The highest-level *anuṣṭhāna* of 2400, 000) *japa sādhanās* of the *Gāyatrī Mantra* under distinct ascetic disciplines).

Prāṇāyāma: An exercise of enhancing and harmonizing the flow of *prāṇa* (vital spiritual energy) within the body through controlled breathing and mental concentration.

Sādhaka: One who sincerely practises a *sādhanā*.

Sādhanā: Devout spiritual endeavor aimed at inner refinement and elevation; it begins with dedicated efforts of self-transformation through control over mind and other senses.

Satsang: Company of good people; attending the discourses and discussions of great personalities.

Swādhyāya: Self-study of enlightening books and self-training through the teachings of elevated souls.

Tapa (tapasyā): Devout austerity, penance and ascetic endeavors of self-purification.

Vanprastha **Ashram** (*Vānaprastha Aśrama*):

> An important stage of life when men and women after fulfilling familial responsibilities would devote themselves full time to service/welfare of the society.

Yagya: Fire ritual. A scientific experiment of vapor-transformation, sublimatization and processing of herbal/plant medicinal preparations in fire in inverted pyramid shaped specifically designs (for slow combustion) with rhythmic chanting of Vedic Mantras.

Yagyashala (*Yagyaśāla*): Especially designed (for performing *yagya*) hall with dome like rooftop standing on pillars in place of walls.